Party
PIECES

The author wearing a party hat, 1940.

Party PIECES

FROM *Do Come* TO *Please Go*

Compiled and edited by
ANNE HARVEY

SUTTON PUBLISHING

First published in the United Kingdom in 2005 by
Sutton Publishing Limited · Phoenix Mill
Thrupp · Stroud · Gloucestershire · GL5 2BU

British Library Cataloguing in Publication Data
A catalogue record for this book is available from the British
Library.

ISBN 0-7509-4142-1

Typeset in 11/16.5pt Sabon.
Typesetting and origination by
Sutton Publishing Limited.
Printed and bound in England by
J.H. Haynes & Co. Ltd, Sparkford.

DEDICATION

An Invitation . . .

to all who have been to my parties

&

to all who have invited me to theirs

&

to all who would rather read about parties

than go to them

&

especially for my friend

Richard Furstenheim

a source of inspiration and a great helper at parties.

CONTENTS

INTRODUCTION

Giving a party is very like making an anthology. Choices must be made: who to invite? what sort of a party? and what time? As with party guests, the contents of an anthology must mix well. A poem that complements or echoes a piece of prose is like introducing two guests to each other, then awaiting the outcome. I had to drop some of the 'possible guests' due to lack of space, and finally chose those from the nineteenth century to the present day who had written about parties that I *might* have enjoyed, plus those I would far rather have missed – though liked reading about.

When I began planning *Party Pieces* a few 'must haves' came to the fore, one being Noel Coward's 'Marvellous Party', that epitome of parties where guests are out of control and all ends in chaos. I must admit to never having been at such a party, but the song makes me feel I was there.

I have, though, been at many literary parties, publishing events and launches and know all about the networking described in *Bridget Jones's Diary*. You always know when your head is being glanced over (not difficult in my case!) for a more useful contact across the crowded room.

'To travel hopefully is a better thing than to arrive,' said Robert Louis Stevenson, and this could apply to party-going. You might start out feeling like 'the hostess with the mostest', but as problems arise, the mood changes, and by the time the first guest appears your heart is sinking. There are endless books on entertaining to aid the nervous (Helen Lederer's advice on page 3 is uplifting), but in the end it all boils down to basics: good food and drink, enough of them, plus the right mix of interesting people.

Difficult guests can mar any occasion and you will meet some within these pages. Joyce Grenfell's Cousin Caroline (who sings) for one, Simon Brett's Little Sod, the Lady who always talks too much, and Uncle Bernard with his puppet show in Alan Ayckbourn's 'Season's Greetings' – all should be struck off the party list.

When I was a child the annual birthday party was a serious affair, particularly over the important matter of GAMES. These took days to organise. Pencils had to be sharpened, records got ready for the gramophone, labels neatly printed for that warm-up game OPPOSITES so that OBERON could find TITANIA, FISH meet CHIPS and so on. You will see (page 127) that Arthur Marshall knew this game too.

A favourite game was ADVERTS, one I think no longer played. Adverts had to be cut out of magazines, then the give-away words – GUINNESS, START-RITE, HEINZ – removed, before the adverts were displayed for guests to decipher. And we always played the TRAY GAME. This first appeared in Kipling's *Kim* to increase the young hero's powers of observation and aid his memory. Baden-Powell included instructions for KIM'S GAME in his hand-book *Scouting for Boys*:

Place about 20 or 30 small articles on a tray, such as buttons, pencils, corks, nuts, stones, knives, string, anything you can find . . . cover over with cloth or a coat. Make a list of these and make a column opposite list for each boy's replies. Then uncover articles for one minute by your watch or while you count 60 at the rate of 'quick march'. Then cover up again.

Take each boy separately and let him whisper to you each of the articles he can remember, and mark it off on your scoring sheet. . . . The boy who remembers the greatest number wins the game.

We still play this at grown-up parties (without the marching or whispers). The Boy Scouts were also responsible for teaching my brother John the Australian ballad 'Waltzing Matilda', which he famously rendered in its entirety at one family party. Like Tennyson's brook (and like Lynne Truss's performance of 'The Highwayman' (see page 123)), it 'went on for ever'.

I was a veteran performer of party pieces inspired by my paternal grandmother, an ardent reciter of parlour poetry, and my maternal grandfather, who was a music-hall entertainer in his youth, boasting the playbill motto 'Always a success without vulgarity'. I have tried not to let him down, and think he would have approved of my presentation of the heart-rending 'Johnnie! You and Me', which you can find among the 'dinner parties'.

When the current rage for football, bowling, swimming and McDonalds parties dies down, maybe old-fashioned traditional parties, like the one in Betjeman's nostalgic 'Indoor Games near Newbury', will stage a comeback. Fashions do go in circles. Who would have guessed that, to be really in the swim today, you must be seen at, or give, a knitting party! It is true, here and in America, and I saw a book on knitting that opened with the line: 'It's my party and I'll knit if I want to!' Obviously a take on that song 'It's my party and I'll cry if I want to!'

Perhaps some readers *have* cried at their own party; certainly some of these writers have felt like crying. For such a convivial subject there is a fair share of doom and gloom. My editor said, 'Keep it light hearted and humorous.' Well, I tried, but I found that many guests (*a*) would rather stay at home (*b*) did not enjoy themselves once there and (*c*) agreed with Jane Austen that 'The sooner every party breaks up the better.'

In Virginia Woolf's novel *Mrs Dalloway*, one character says of another: 'Why does she give these parties?'

I would like to hope that none of my friends asks such a question after my annual party, despite being coerced into games ('guests must join in even if they don't feel like it') and, of course, being asked to perform their 'party pieces'.

Anne Harvey
April 2005

LET'S HAVE A PARTY

Said Mr Podsnap to Mrs Podsnap, 'Georgiana is almost eighteen.'

Said Mrs Podsnap to Mr Podsnap, assenting, 'Almost eighteen.'

Said Mr Podsnap then to Mrs Podsnap, 'Really I think we should have some people on Georgiana's birthday.'

Said Mrs Podsnap then to Mr Podsnap, 'Which will enable us to clear off all those people who are due.'

Charles Dickens, *Our Mutual Friend*, 1864–5

from The History Man

Malcolm Bradbury

Now it is the Autumn again; the people are all coming back. Some people called Kirk, a well-known couple, decide to have a party. . . . they set to work at once on the who, what and how of it. Howard leaves their bright pine kitchen and goes out into the hall to fetch, from beside their busy telephone, their busy house diary, a crucial text and record for people like themselves.

'When?' says Barbara. 'Soon,' says Howard. 'Are we free on the first day of term?' asks Barbara. It is improbable, but Howard turns the pages; there is the day, Monday 2nd October, and the evening is a blank. It is almost an omen, and Howard writes, in his neat little hand, as if writing the start of some new story, which in a sense is what it is, the word PARTY in the small space of white on the crowded page.

from Miss Manners' Guide to Excruciatingly Correct Behaviour

Dear Miss Manners
   Do you have to invite the same number of men as women or does it matter if you have more of one sex or the other?

Gentle Reader
   It depends on what sort of activity you are inviting them to engage in. If the activity is to be conventional, it doesn't matter.

from Coping: How to Get the Better of Life

Helen Lederer

PARTIES

Given the right preparation and the necessary relaxed attitude there is no reason why your parties shouldn't be as successful as mine. All you need to do is pay attention to details, such as inviting people, buying drink and remembering to be in on the night. Getting the right mix and number of people is vital. You cannot always assume that everyone you invite will turn up – I usually allow for a 90 per cent drop-out rate. A correctly worded, pleasantly set-out invitation is likely to increase your chances:

Helen invites you to a

PARTY

8.00 *Saturday November 10th*

Bring a bottle

Please come to my party (but only if you want to). I promise the drink won't run out this time and there won't be any of that paella that seemed to repeat rather unpleasantly throughout the evening. And there will be other people there.

So please come on the 10th if you can make it; if you can't, it'll be on the 19th, or possibly the 27th if that will be more convenient, or maybe you think I shouldn't have one at all which is fine, just let me know and I'll cancel the whole thing.

Oh, and if you're the person who threw up on the sofa perhaps you'd like to eat before you arrive this time (the cushions came up very well considering).

R.S.P.C.A.

3

You may feel reluctant to hold a party because you are frightened of what people will think of your home. I know just how you feel – guests tend to make snap judgements which can take months of persuasion to dispel. An old gonk found underneath a cushion can ruin your credibility and destroy your confidence for the whole evening.

By paying attention to details you can guarantee to create the right impression. I know before I entertain I take time to prepare the ground. A noticeboard full of invitations, a forged love letter peeping out of a book, a few present tags left discreetly around the room, with messages such as 'hope this diamond doesn't offend you', can considerably improve your status.

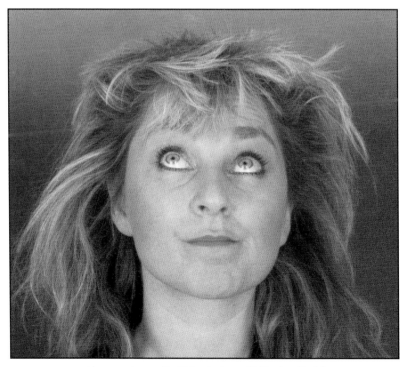

Above and opposite: Helen Lederer. *(© Stephen Hyde)*

Questionnaire

Please fill in this questionnaire for future reference – if it's not too much trouble – so I know whether to bother inviting you again, ever.

1. Do you like me

      a) a lot   ❑
      b) a bit   ❑
      c) indifferent   ❑
      d) not at all?   ❑

2. Did you find my last party

      a) fab   ❑
      b) amazing   ❑
      c) challenging   ❑
      d) other?   ❑

Page 1

Questionnaire *(continued)*

3. Did you find my banana joke

    a) hilarious ❑
    b) offensive ❑
    c) radically altered your
       perception of the fruit/
       man debate? ❑

4. Did you think the fight

    a) brought people together ❑
    b) was my fault for mentioning
       Peter's impotence ❑
    c) encouraged people
       to go home a bit early? ❑

Please do not defecate on this form.

Page 2

from Of a Party

Jan Struther

GIVING a party is very like having a baby: its conception is more fun than its completion, and once you have begun it it is almost impossible to stop. How perfect it is, that first moment, when one of you says, 'It's about time we gave another party,' and suddenly the room is full of people, talking, laughing, drinking, the women all beautiful and the men witty. So rosy is the picture that you lose no time in setting the reality in train. To begin with, a date is chosen – not too near, lest the sought-after people should be already engaged, and not too far ahead, lest your own enthusiasm should flag. Next, the form of invitation has to be considered. It is desirable, you feel, to steer between the copper-plate formality of:

Mr and Mrs Moffat-Grimes At Home

and the self-conscious Bohemianism of 'Jane and Tommy are throwing a party on Thursday week – please come along.' Finally, you decide upon:

Mr and Mrs Moffat-Grimes
invite you to a Party on

. . . .

And you fill in the date on the line below.

After the invitations are posted there is a short respite until the answers begin to come in. It is like a summer shower; first there are a few preliminary drops – people who reply by telephone in order to save time, but who cannot ring off after less than five minutes' chat, during which they demand from

8

you all over again the details of date and hour which you had been so careful to have printed on the invitation. Then, for the next four or five days, comes a spate of letters and post cards. This is the most agreeable time of all: the lover, the party-giver and the free-lance journalist are the only people who feel a genuine interest in the postman's knock. A good deal of gruesome amusement can be got out of taking the first half-dozen acceptances and imagining what would happen if the party were to consist solely of these. They are nearly always of horrifying incompatibility: a couple of brilliant talkers each of whom prefers to be the only brilliant talker in the room, a die-hard colonel, a pacifist poet, a nubile but witless débutante, and a man who has just written a standard work on toads. Supposing – but it is only a nightmare: the worst that can happen is that these six will be the first to arrive.

Presently the spate wanes to a rill, then into detached last-minute driblets full of apologies and exclamation marks. By the morning of the party 90 per cent of your invitations have been answered.

from Miss Manners' Guide to Excruciatingly Correct Behaviour

Dear Miss Manners

I want to issue an invitation to a woman who is living with someone, and to indicate that she may bring him. Should I write . . . 'and GUEST' . . . with her name?

Gentle Reader

Certainly, presuming that his name is Guest. The way to write it is: Miss Alexandra Dashing . . . Mr Theodore Guest . . . If Guest is not his name, then find out what it is.

TEN COMMANDMENTS
For Giving a Successful Party

1. If you must throw a party make up your mind to throw a good one.

2. Invite congenial people who all whoop in the same language.

3. In case of new arrivals, make introductions as informal and general as possible.

4. Plan your party. It should have plenty of action, novelty, and young men.

5. Never put any suggestions to a vote; be sure of the mood of your guests and then go ahead.

6. Know your games but only dip into your repertory for those that will go over big with the time, the place, and the crowd.

7. Remember that a party, like an army, travels on its stomach and be ready with plenty of timely food and drink.

8. When a guest sulks or refuses to join in, ignore him, or her.

9. When two dull people show up, pair them together; it will teach them to snap out of it.

10. If you're not a good leader yourself, be sure to invite some one who is; one live wire will electrify the party.

Some advice from *How to be the Life of the Party*.

Party

Charlotte Mitchell

The invitation said
Bring a guest
which is usually possible.
The difficulty is
To bring yourself –
not the self that got ready
the self that decided what to wear,
the self that set out to go there –
but the other self that has a habit
of staying at home,
or more often
of going to another party of its own,
to which it has forgotten to invite anyone.

from The Diary of a Provincial Lady

E.M. Delafield

October 17th: Surprising invitation to evening party – Dancing, 9.30 – at Lady B.'s. Cannot possibly refuse, as Robert has been told to make himself useful there in various ways; moreover, entire neighbourhood is evidently being polished off, and see no object in raising question as to whether we have, or have not, received invitation. Decide to get new dress, but must have it made locally, owing to rather sharply worded enquiry from London shop which has the privilege of serving me, as to

whether I have not overlooked overdue portion of account? (Far from overlooking it, have actually been kept awake by it at night.) Proceed to Plymouth, and get very attractive black taffeta, with little pink and blue posies scattered over it. Mademoiselle removes, and washes, Honiton lace from old purple velvet every-night tea-gown, and assures me that it will be *gentil à croquer* on new taffeta. Also buy new pair black evening-shoes, but shall wear them every evening for at least an hour in order to ensure reasonable comfort at party.

The Extra Man

Cole Porter

In the infinite variety of men who make up society
I'm quite the most pathetic of all the clan.
For amongst the gay unthinking set,
The heavy eating and drinking set,
I'm commonly known as an extra man.
If a hostess's voice is hearty
When inviting me to a party,
I accept although I know what it's all about.

For I realize I'm the buddy
Who's elected to understudy
Some boyfriend who's suddenly given out.
I'm an extra man, an extra man.
I've got no equal as an extra man.
I'm handsome, I'm harmless, I'm helpful, I'm able,
A perfect fourth at bridge or a
 fourteenth at table.
You will find my name
 on ev'ry list,
But when it's missing it
 is never missed.
And so I'll live until
 that fatal day,
The press will tell you
 that I've passed
 away.
And you will feel sad
 as the news you
 scan
For that means
 one less extra
 man.

from The History Man

Malcolm Bradbury

The Kirks always do have good parties, have a talent for giving them . . . they are unstructured parties, frames for events . . . the principle is creative mixture. So the Kirks are mixing people from the town with people from the University, and people from London with people from the town. They are mixing heteros with homos, painters with advanced theologians, scientists with historians, students with Hell's Angels, pop stars with IRA supporters . . . the Kirks have a wide intellectual constituency, an expansive acquaintance . . . 'I think we're losing spontaneity,' says Howard. 'We said an unpredictable encounter.' 'I just want to ask,' says Barbara, 'how many people we'll have at this unpredictable encounter. I'm thinking about the work.' 'We have to make it a real scene,' says Howard. 'A hundred, maybe more.' 'Your idea of a good party', says Barbara, 'is to invite the universe. And then leave me to wash up after.' 'Oh, come on,' says Howard. 'We need this. They need it.' 'Your enthusiasm,' says Barbara, 'it never wears does it?' 'Right,' says Howard. 'That's why I exist. Now I'm going to pick up the telephone and make twenty-five calls and then you're going to make twenty-five calls, and there's our party.'

from Bridget Jones's Diary

Helen Fielding

TUESDAY 11 APRIL

8st 11, alcohol units 0, cigarettes 0, Instants 9 (this must stop).

Am invited to a glittering literati launch of *Kafka's Motorbike* next week at the Ivy. Determined, instead of fearing the scary party, panicking all the way through and going home pissed and depressed, am going to improve social skills, confidence and Make Parties Work for Me – as guided by article have just read in magazine.

Apparently, Tina Brown of the *New Yorker* is brilliant at dealing with parties, gliding gently from group to group, saying, 'Martin Amis! Nelson Mandela! Richard Gere!' in a tone which at once suggests, 'My God, I have never been more enchanted to see anyone in my entire life! Have you met the most dazzling person at the party apart from you? Talk! Talk! Must network! Byeee!' Wish to be like Tina Brown, though not, obviously, quite as hardworking.

The article is full of useful tips. One should never, apparently, talk to anyone at a party for more than two minutes. When time is up, you simply say, 'I think we're expected to circulate. Nice to meet you,' and go off. If you get lost for words after asking someone what they do to which they reply 'Undertaker' or 'I work for the Child Support Agency', you must simply ask, 'Do you enjoy that?' When introducing people add a thoughtful detail or two about each person so that their interlocutor has a conversational kicking-off point. E.g., 'This is John – he's from New Zealand and enjoys windsurfing.' Or, 'Gina is a keen skydiver and lives on a barge.'

Let's Have a Party

Most importantly, one must never go to a party without a clear objective: whether it be to 'network', thereby adding to your spread of contacts to improve your career; to make friends with someone specific; or simply 'clinch' a top deal. Understand where have been going wrong by going to parties armed only with objective of not getting too pissed.

from Miss Manners' Guide to Excruciatingly Correct Behaviour

A Correct R.s.v.p.

Dear Miss Manners

Which is correct, 'R.S.V.P.' or 'R.s.v.p.' I have seen both on properly engraved invitations.

Gentle Reader

If Miss Manners told you all the improprieties she has seen on allegedly properly engraved invitations, it would curl your hair. 'R.s.v.p.' is correct. It stands for the imperative sentence 'Répondez, s'il vous plaît.' If you were to write this in English, you would put, 'Kindly give an answer', not 'Kindly Give Me an Answer.' Possibly you would put 'KINDLY GIVE ME AN ANSWER!' but Miss Manners does not believe in shouting.

'Répondez, s'il vous plaît'

Dear Miss Manners

I disagree with your use of 'R.s.v.p.' '*Répondez, s'il vous plait*' is not 'Kindly give me an answer,' but 'Respond if you please.' Therefore, saying 'If you please' leaves it up to the recipient to respond or not. So, in fact, using R.s.v.p. means you can either inform the sender, or not. Does this mean the use of R.s.v.p. is a waste of time? Also, what about the few who know the proper meaning of R.s.v.p. – are they to be condemned if they don't respond!

Gentle Reader

The surest way to be condemned socially is to take conventional phrases literally. 'S'il vous plaît' indeed means 'if you please', but there is no option about complying. Try responding literally to such conventional phrases as 'How do you do?' 'Please make yourself at home', and 'Feel free to call me any time if there is anything I can do for you', and see how far you get. If there is doubt that your prospective guests will understand 'R.s.v.p.' you may just as correctly write, 'The favour of a reply is requested'.

from The One I Knew the Best of All

Frances Hodgson Burnett

Each time that a note arrived 'hoping to have the pleasure' of her company – and that of her sisters and brothers – wild exhilaration reigned. Everybody began to be excited at once. A party seemed a thing it was impossible to wait patiently for. It got into one's head and one's body, and made one dance about instead of walking. I do not think this resulted from anticipation of the polkas and games or the negus and tipsy-cake, or was absolutely a consequence of the prospect of donning the white frock and sash and slippers – it was the Party that did it. Perhaps young birds who have just learned to fly, young ducks in their first plunge into a pond, young chanticleers who have discovered they can crow, may feel something of the same elation and delight. It was the Party!

THE COCKTAIL PARTY

Easily the best advice about giving a cocktail party is . . .
DON'T!

Kenneth Horne, *Woman's Hour Cookery Book*

The Darkest Half-hour . . . or,
Too Early is the Time for all Good Guests
to Come to the Aid of the Party

Ogden Nash

They are ready for their party.

And by 7.05 they are in the livingroom, poised, braced,
anticipatory and on the qui vive.

Eagerly they await the doorbell, or in certain climes,
The ripple of those melodious Wistful Vista chimes.

He starts to light a cigarette, but she halts him with
gestures frenzied –
The ashtrays have just been cleansèd.

She starts to sit on the sofa, and he, the most impartial
umpire who ever umped,
Evens the count by reminding her that the sofa has just
been plumped.

Then she divides the number of olives by the number of
guests and hopes she has not been too frugal.

And wishes that the caviar were not the sticky reddish kind
but genuinely Belugal.

By 7.25 she is pacing the floor and nibbling at her finger-
nails, destroying the opalescent symmetry acquired at
the afternoon manicure,

And he inquires, 'Are you sure it was this Saturday and not
next that you asked them for?'
– a question not recommended as the ideal panic cure.

At 7.30 they are tense as mummers awaiting rise of the
curtain, and at 7.31 they have abandoned their
mumming –
They are convinced that no-one is coming.

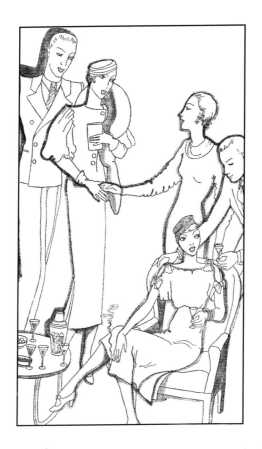

So he says how about a quick one, and just as he has one
hand on the ice bucket and the other on the gin,
Why, the first couple walks in.

Throwing a Party

Elsa Maxwell

The cocktail party is the worst invention since castor oil. I've
never given a cocktail party. You know what usually happens.
The condemned couple greet you at the door with a clammy
hand and a despairing eye. They know better than anyone the
torture to be inflicted on you. They can't accommodate all the

people who have been invited and each new arrival means so many more decibels of noise and so many more gallons of noxious cigarette smoke. Everyone is screaming and smoking in self-defence. The limp anchovies on soggy biscuits are an offence to your stomach and are compounded by luke-warm prefabricated drink. The hostess anxiously wonders how many diehards will hang on to the bitter end in the delusion that dinner is to be served. The host wonders how long his liquor and ice will hold out and decides to make deep inroads in both in the hope that everyone will go home when nothing is left to drink. Eventually, and not a moment too soon, the condemned couple are reprieved by the fatigue that drives their guests into the night in search of a place to sit down.

from A Positively Final Appearance

Alec Guinness

Alec Guinness was in Manhattan in 1951, playing in T.S. Eliot's The Cocktail Party. *Elsa Maxwell, whom he described as 'the ugly dumpy New York café society hostess', invited the company to supper.*

'Let's get out of here before worse befalls,' I said to a couple from *The Cocktail Party*. 'There is bound to be a drugstore near by where we can have eggs, sunny-side-up.' We didn't bother with our hostess but just got ourselves out of the building.

Poor Elsa Maxwell: she had a nasty tumble towards the end of her enterprising career. The world understood (through innumerable photographs in the glossies) that she had a close relationship with the Windsors over several years, but then there came a tiff and the swishing aside of skirts. A reconciliation was brought about in mid-Atlantic during very bad weather. The Duchess invited her to a cocktail party in the Windsor stateroom. On arrival Maxwell attempted a deep curtsy, which unfortunately coincided with a roll of the ship. Maxwell tumbled over, clutching at the Windsor legs, which took erratic steps sideways. The cries of 'Wallis!' 'Elsa!' were muffled in the sound of crashing glass.

from The Cocktail Party

T.S. Eliot

EDWARD. I like the dress you're wearing:
I'm glad you put on that one.

LAVINIA. Well, Edward!
Do you know it's the first time you've paid me a compliment
Before a party? And that's when one needs them.

EDWARD. Well, you deserve it. – We asked too many people.

LAVINIA. It's true, a great many more accepted
Than we thought would want to come. But what can you do?
There's usually a lot who don't want to come
But all the same would be bitterly offended
To hear we'd given a party without asking them.

EDWARD. Perhaps we ought to have arranged to have two parties
Instead of one.

LAVINIA.   That's never satisfactory.
Everyone who's asked to either party
Suspects that the other one was more important.

EDWARD. That's true. You have a very practical mind.

LAVINIA. But you know, I don't think that you need worry:
They won't all come, out of those who accepted.
You know we said, 'we can ask twenty more
Because they will be going to the Gunnings instead'.

EDWARD. I know, that's what we said at the time;
But I'd forgotten what the Gunnings' parties were like.
Their guests will get just enough to make them thirsty;
They'll come on to us later, roaring for drink.
Well, let's hope that those who come to us early
Will be going on to the Gunnings afterwards,
To make room for those who come from the Gunnings.

THEATRE ROYAL HAYMARKET

THE COCKTAIL PARTY

BY

T. S. ELIOT

Programme

First Performance at this Theatre
Monday, February 3rd 1969
First Performance at Wyndhams Theatre
Wednesday, November 6th 1968

LAVINIA. And if it's very crowded, they can't get at the
   cocktails,
And the man won't be able to take the tray about,
So they'll go away again. Anyway, at that stage
There's nothing whatever you can do about it:
And everyone likes to be seen at a party
Where everybody else is, to show they've been invited.
That's what makes it a success. Is that picture straight?
EDWARD. Yes, it is.
LAVINIA.   No, it isn't. Do please straighten it.
EDWARD. Is it straight now?
LAVINIA.   Too much to the left.
EDWARD. How's that now?
LAVINIA.   No, I meant the right.
   That will do. I'm too tired to bother.
EDWARD. After they're all gone, we will have some champagne,
   Just ourselves. You lie down now, Lavinia
   No one will be coming for at least half an hour;
   So just stretch out.
LAVINIA.   You must sit beside me,
   Then I can relax.
EDWARD.   This is the best moment
   Of the whole party.
LAVINIA.   Oh no, Edward.
   The best moment is the moment it's over;
   And then to remember, it's the end of the season
   And no more parties.

The Cocktail Party

Judith Viorst

The hostess is passing the sour-cream dip and the carrots, and
The husband is mixing up something with rum in the blender, and
The mothers are finishing teething and starting on ear aches, and
The ones with the tan are describing their trip to St Thomas, and
The fellow they swore was funnier than Joey Bishop
Is discussing tax breaks
With the fellow they swore was funnier than Mort Sahl, and
The hostess is passing the eggs with the mayonnaise-curry, and
The husband is being risqué with a blonde in the foyer, and
The mothers are finishing ear aches and starting on day camps, and
The one who can play the piano is playing Deep Purple, and
The fellow they swore was smarter than David Susskind
Is discussing field goals

The country cousin (a student of the fashion papers)
who thought she was correctly attired for a cocktail party.

With the fellow they swore was smarter than Max Lerner, and
The hostess is passing the heat-and-serve pigs-in-a-blanket, and
The husband is passing out cold on the coats in the bedroom, and
The mothers are finishing day camps and starting on sex play, and
The one on the diet is saying she's not even hungry, and
The fellow they swore was cuter than Warren Beatty
Is discussing drain pipes
With the fellow they swore was cuter than Michael Caine, and
I'm not as out of place
As I wish I were.

from Best Behaviour

Mary Killen

HOW TO GET AWAY FROM
PEOPLE AT A DRINKS PARTY

Q. How can I move on at a drinks party without appearing to
be rude?

M.G.C., Inverness

A. *Gradually and imperceptibly allow the space between you
and your interlocutor to become larger. Meantime allow a
vague expression to pass over your face. Soon others will
start to push through the gap, assuming it is a passageway.
Having lost contact, it should be easy for you to slip away.
Alternatively, on greeting each interlocutor, state that you are
worried about your car which you have parked badly. After a
while you can easily say, 'I must go and check my car'.*

from Say Please: Cocktail Parties

Virginia Graham

A lady who only knows her husband at a cocktail party need not be too depressed, for although it may seem rather a waste of time to dress up in a drinking costume in order to stand in a crowd and talk to him, many husbands and wives have had extraordinarily interesting conversations in such circumstances. Forced by the rules of etiquette to appear animated and even happy, they have abandoned their usual topics of talk, consisting as they so frequently do of queries regarding temporal matters which can be answered monosyllabically or merely by optic implication, and have plunged into subjects on

GUESTS WE WILL NEVER INVITE AGAIN

The cocktail-party guests who won't go—and you have your own party to go to.

which since their engagements they have had no time or desire to ponder; subjects such as God, Existentialism, Stamp Collecting and so forth.

At the end of a cocktail party there are always two or three people who will not or cannot go. Embedded in a sofa like roots of oak trees in the earth they remain, smiling benevolently out on to the scene of devastation and saying '*Lovely* party, darling. The *greatest* fun'. It is not always easy to gain access to the minds of these fuddled derelicts, but if such remarks as 'Do have another drink before you GO?' or 'Now the party's OVER and NOBODY else is coming, do finish off the radishes!' have no effect, a hostess may strive to speed the undeparting guests by taking off her shoes and ostentatiously emptying the ashtrays, collecting the glasses, and carrying them all away into the kitchen. If this somewhat drastic procedure is unavailing it can safely be assumed that what is sitting on the sofa is stewed. Pickled guests should either be left where they are or, if they are conscious, should be led gently down the stairs and put into a hastily summoned vehicle. From no lady's cocktail party should a guest ever be *carried*. Any lady who has friends liable to be called for by ambulances is no lady. She is just a woman who shouldn't give cocktail parties.

My Oxford

Anthony Thwaite

. . . memories of vomiting blindly from
small Tudor windows

Philip Larkin, *All What Jazz*

Trinity Term – From somewhere down the High
A gramophone enunciates its wish
To put another nickel in, and I
Am going to have drinks with Ernle-Fyshe,
A Merton man who had a poem once
In *Time and Tide*. The future has begun.
Over by Magdalen Bridge the tethered punts
Knock at the jetty. I am having fun.

Upstairs I hand my bottle over, take
A mug of rhubarb-coloured punch, and wave
A sprightly hand at someone. 'I just make
Whatever's made from what you bring.' A grave
Critic from Keble, aged nineteen, says why
The only man is Mauriac. And then
A girl in peasant dirndl, dark and shy,
Asks me to tell her about Origen.

My bow-tie chaste, my waistcoat green brocade,
I lay the law down, and another drink.
Bells clang from colleges, her hair is swayed
By breezes at the open window. Think
How much there is to do (that villanelle,
That *Isis* piece, that essay for A4) –
But confidently thinking all is well
I gulp another, sinking to the floor.

Someone recites his latest poem, while
Tom Lehrer's lyrics sidle through the haze.
'What John Crowe Ransom has is purely style.'
'Auden is only passing through a phase.'
The girl has turned elsewhere. My head goes round.
Let Mauriac and co. do what they like.
I lean from the embrasure. There's the sound
Of copious liquid drenching someone's bike.

O Golden Age! O Nineteen Fifty-Three,
When the whole world lay wide in front of me!

from Complete Guide to Gatecrashing

Nicholas Allan

*I feel privileged to have for a friend a professional gatecrasher.
In his* Complete Guide to Gatecrashing *Nicholas Allan offers
invaluable advice on this activity. For example, the gatecrasher
should not look like one. A good black suit is recommended,
preferably an Armani. He advocates that you*

DRESS FOR SUCCESS

It is always advantageous to dress well, even if you're just
visiting the corner shop for a Mars Bar. At a routine
appointment at my local hospital, I noticed a champagne
reception and buffet about to begin in the main atrium. I
hurried to my appointment, then joined the party after as a
visiting consultant.

MY FIRST TIME

I'll never forget it.

I was at the Royal Festival Hall to attend a tedious concert – Brahm's *Requiem*, probably – in which a friend was participating. Arriving early, I noticed people entering the inappropriately named 'People's Palace Restaurant' (it is expensive), which had been cleared of tables for a party. Trays of champagne were floating; a flunky stood with one by the door.

'Are you with the party, suh?' The tray swooped.

'Yes, but I'm waiting for a friend.'

'Would you care for a glass while you're waiting, suh?'

Taking a glass, I held it disbelievingly, took my first sip – and never looked back. The glass was a party invitation card. Soon I was standing by the windowed wall, waiting patiently for the hot buffet supper, looking out on a moonlit Thames, and beyond, over a Never-Never Land of winking lights below a turquoise sky, each light beckoning, each light a promise of another party like this. It was an epiphany, the discovery of a

case of buried banknotes. This is how the Brink's-Mat Bank Robbers felt driving home. I'd accidentally dropped into Aladdin's cave: the world, I suddenly realised, was my party. If gatecrashing is an addiction, like smoking or shoplifting – which is exactly how it turned out to be for me – I was hooked.

from Best Behaviour

Mary Killen

HOW TO GET RID OF PEOPLE
AT THE END OF A DRINK'S PARTY

Q. I love giving drinks parties, with one reservation. I like to collapse afterwards but I find that certain of one's friends and contacts will always stay on well beyond the time stipulated for departure on their invitation. These are generally people who have been inefficient about making arrangements for dinner and so are left at something of a loose end when everyone else goes off.

They then stay on, spinning out the rest of the evening by eating crisps and peanuts. Then one hears them ask, 'You haven't got a slice of bread I could have?' rather accusingly.

How can one effect the departure of late-staying guests?

B.R., Eaton Place

A. *Although you say you like to collapse after such an occasion, many hostesses in your position would be expected to go out to dinner themselves. Therefore, at a moment when you are satisfied that enough has been enough, you should put on your coat and tell those guests who are remaining: 'I've got a dinner date, but do please stay on. The only thing is that, if*

Original Suits for the Cocktail Hour.

EXCLUSIVE MODEL LOUNGE PYJAMA carried out in navy, red and beige crepe-de-chine, and comprising red trousers, beige sleeveless jumper, or can be worn as a tuck-in blouse, trimmed diagonal bands of navy and red crepe-de-chine. A most original three-quarter length coat which is three coats in one, each one in a different colour, surmounting the other.

Price complete **12½** gns.

DELIGHTFUL THREE PIECE SMOKING PYJAMA carried out in crepe-de-chine featuring an autumnal colour scheme. The deep leaf green stitched three-quarter coat surmounts an amber jumper trimmed diagonal bands of orange, or can be worn as the new tuck-in blouse, wide orange trousers complete a charming ensemble for informal occasions.

Price complete **8½** gns.

MARSHALL & SNELGROVE
Debenham Limited
VERE STREET & OXFORD STREET :: :: LONDON, W.1

you are going to stay on, then I must give someone the responsibility of turning off the burglar alarm, so who is going to be the last person to leave, because that would be the most sensible person to do it?'

You will find that the late-stayers will rise, as a man, from their trays of peanuts, saying, 'Oh, it won't be me. I must go now'.

DINNER AT EIGHT

`I really take it very kind,
This visit, Mrs Skinner!
I have not seen you such an age – `
(The wretch has come to dinner!)

Thomas Hood, *Domestic Asides*

from Kitchen Essays

Agnes Jekyll

THEIR FIRST DINNER-PARTY

The first dinner-party is always an interesting event in a newly-founded home, and should be so organized as not to monopolize the attention of host and hostess to the exclusion of social enjoyment. It must not err on the side of parsimony, nor yet by its lavishness vex those new relations or old aunts whose attitude has been aptly characterized as 'affectionate, but hostile'. 'Not fewer in number than the Graces, nor yet exceeding the Muses,' runs an old adage regarding the perfect party; so, avoiding both danger points, let the table be well and truly laid for eight cheerful guests. All beginnings are important. If you can establish a name for having good food by a series of successful hospitalities, friends will grow lyrical over your cold mutton, and even ask for the recipe of the Shepherd's Pie – so potent and mysterious are the workings of suggestion! On that principle oysters or caviare might well be ordered to head the first menu, but they are costly additions, and, as George Meredith was wont to say, 'Economy, our dread old friend, must decide!'

> Hospitality has nothing to do with money. Some of the best hosts I know invariably have their parties paid for by somebody else.
>
> *(Country Life)*

from Miss Manners' Guide to Excrutiatingly Correct Behaviour

SEATING ARRANGEMENTS

Dear Miss Manners

Last night we went to a dinner party at the home of some neighbours we've never visited before. They have a big dining room, and it was all fixed up with candles and everything, so I asked the hostess where I should sit. She said, 'Oh, just sit anywhere,' and so I did. Then the host said, 'No, I'm sitting there' – it was a sort of oval table, so I couldn't tell what was to be the head of it – so I moved. I picked another place, but then we were told to get up to get our food from the buffet table, and somebody else sat down in that place. So then I took my plate and sat down again – you notice that this is now the third time I've tried to sit down and have dinner – and guess who comes and sits next to me! My wife. I know married couples aren't supposed to sit next to each other at dinners, but I didn't know she'd been sitting there and was now up getting her plate filled. I got fed up when the hostess noticed where I was and said, 'Oh, you two can't sit next to each other,' and my wife sat there as if she wasn't ever going to move. But I still was nice, and I said, 'OK, where do you want me to sit?' and the hostess said, 'Oh, sit anywhere,' and when I looked at her – this is now the third time she or her husband had made me move – she said, 'I mean anywhere else.' So I took my plate and went and sat in the living room. Would you mind telling me what the hell 'Sit anywhere' means?

Gentle Reader

It means that the hostess has not taken the trouble to finish planning her dinner party. If the hostess cannot carry the seating arrangement in her head so that she can give you a decent answer to your decent question of where you should sit, she ought to use place cards.

from The Essential Handbook
of Victorian Etiquette

BEHAVIOUR TO BE AVOIDED AT THE TABLE

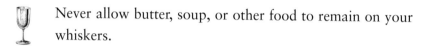 Never allow butter, soup, or other food to remain on your whiskers.

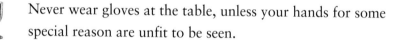 Never wear gloves at the table, unless your hands for some special reason are unfit to be seen.

Never, when serving others, overload the plate nor force upon them delicacies which they decline.

Never make a display when removing hair, insects, or other disagreeable things from your food. Place them quietly under the edge of your plate.

Place Settings

Jeremy Nicholas

Sheila's next to Andrew
And Andrew's opposite Marge,
Sarah can have the window seat
Because she's rather large.
Clive can flirt with Kay
So put Sally on the right,
Kath must be with Ian
'Cos he's bound to end up tight.
Edward can go in the corner,
I'm sure he wouldn't mind.
Bill can talk the pants off Jim,
Let Joy be unconfined.
Dorothy's a problem
Because she's such a bitch.
On the other hand,
She's very old and very rich.

Susan has decided
She's going to come with Kim
And Bertram is insisting
That we put him next to Tim.
Philip and his girlfriend
Won't come with any luck.
They've got so much in common,
Yes, they're both as common as muck!
Simon can cope with Nicky
As long as she's not near Ted,
So we'd better put Ken with Antonia
After what Elspeth said.

" And now they want another place at table for Henry, Earl of Bolcester, whoever he *is !"*

But Dorothy's a problem,
She's such a frightful bore.
Her cystitis is still playing up,
So put her near the door.

Jill has rung to tell me
That she fancies Dick,
But Rachel says he might not come –
Doesn't it make you sick!
Can we ask the Wilsons?
Would it be all right

If we took them into the garden
And kept them out of sight?
Eric, Wayne and Karlene
Will have to sit next to their Mum.
As long as I'm nowhere near them
We'd better let them come.
But Dorothy's a problem,
She's got an awful thirst.
She eats us out of house and home
And always gets here first.

Martin's next to Tina
And Tina's such a tease.
Keep her away from Elizabeth
Or it's sure to upset Louise.
Cyril and Natasha
Have said they'll try and show,
But they don't get on with David,
Richard, Angela or Joe.
Jean-Pierre and Martina
Are flying in from France.
Shall we leave a place for them
Or shall we take a chance?
But Dorothy's a problem,
She's coming on her own.
Reg put up with her last time,
Let's give her Aunty Joan.

I think that's everybody,
There's you and me and Ben.
Oh wait! We've left out Anthony!
We'll have to start again . . .

from Miss Manners' Guide to Excruciatingly Correct Behaviour

Dear Miss Manners

The doctor and I have a pleasant bantering relationship and I think I would enjoy seeing him socially. Is it all right for me to extend a dinner party invitation to him?

Gentle Reader

Only if you do so with your clothes on.

from Below Stairs

Margaret Powell

Although I was now quite expert (as a cook), it was a good job I had never taken up any other part of domestic service like being a parlourmaid and waiting at table. I only had one experience of it and that was enough. One evening Mrs Bishop was giving a dinner party and Hilda was taken ill and couldn't wait at table. Mrs Bishop came rushing down to me to ask if I could come in between the courses and help hand things round. The housemaid was to do the silver serving, and I was to hand the vegetables round. I knew I would suffer agonies of embarrassment. You can just imagine coming up from the heat of the kitchen with a face like a peony and wearing a print dress into the bargain. When I arrived in the dining-room Mrs Bishop announced to the company at large, 'This is my cook.' Well, of course, everybody gaped at me, which didn't help, I felt like Exhibit A. One of the vegetables was tiny little new potatoes, they looked very attractive in the dish on the silver salver, with mint and butter sauce – piping hot they were too. The first guest I had to serve was an attractive Frenchwoman.

Well, I was so nervous my hand started shaking like a leaf – the dish shot down the salver and all these marble-sized new potatoes shot all down her front and her lap. She jumped up and let out a stream of French words I couldn't understand. Then I saw that one of the potatoes had got lodged in her cleavage – so I tried to get it out with the serving spoon. The silly thing didn't keep still – it must have been burning her – anyway instead of getting it out I squashed it against her breast. She flung the spoon out of my hand and screamed, 'Coshon, coshon' about half a dozen times. Talk about *Oliver Twist*, but she didn't ask for more. I fled downstairs.

HOSTESS OF DINNER-PARTY: "ANY SIGN OF DINNER YET?"
MAID: "NO, MA'AM—AND COOK SAYS SHE'D LIKE TO SEE YOU FOR A MINUTE BEFORE SHE GOES."

from Period Piece: A Cambridge Childhood

Gwen Raverat

In Period Piece: A Cambridge Childhood *Gwen Raverat writes
of the dinner parties given by her parents. She kept some
menus. Here is one for 'clearly rather a grand dinner'
on 31 October 1885:*

Clear Soup
Brill and Lobster Sauce
Chicken Cutlets and Rice Balls
Oyster Patties
Mutton, Potatoes, Artichokes, Beets
Partridges and Salad
Caramel Pudding }
Pears and Whipped Cream }
Cheese Ramequins }
Cheese Straws }
Ice
Grapes, Walnuts, Chocolates and Pears.

But she did not enjoy her first grown up dinner party, when she was 18.

As I grew older, parties grew steadily worse. My mother saw
that we were shy and bad mixers, and thought that seeing more
people would be good for us; and so, in our adolescence, she
grew more and more autocratic about forcing us to go out. Of
course, she was perfectly right in principle, only it did not work
out well in practice.

It was a difficult situation both for her and for me. The kind of
girl she understood was gay and pretty and charming, and had
lots of love-affairs and told her all about them; and she never
understood that I could not – really *could* not – fill this role.

I am certain that she never understood the agonies I went through. Shyness was so alien to her that she could not take it seriously, and could only laugh at me, or scold me mildly, which made me feel guilty as well as shy. 'It is so *silly*!' [Of course it was, I knew that perfectly well, but it didn't make any difference.] 'People can't eat you!' [No, but *look* at you, which was much worse.]

She could never have believed it possible that it was out of uncontrollable panic that I upset a whole dish of spinach into my lap, at one of the first dinner-parties I ever went to. I was about eighteen, and I had on my best green satin evening dress, very smart and tight and shiny. I mopped away at the mess with my long white kid gloves, and made it much worse. The kind parlour-maid tried to help me; but my neighbours, instead of making a joke of it, pretended that they did not see; no doubt from the best of motives, but it was not the right treatment. Oh dear, Oh dear, how I did wish to fall down dead that very instant! But it was a horrible dress anyhow; I had been allowed no choice in colour or make; and I was glad when it was found to be spoilt for ever.

Dinner Party

Virginia Graham

The flushed faces are lit by candles on the table,
Cigar ash on the Worcester, scent on the sable,
'What are we arguing about?' 'How did it all start?'
'I hate you, I hate you from the bottom of my heart!'
'Silly young puppy!' 'What do *you* know of the Law?'
'Why not admit, dear, you've never read any of Shaw?'

'All small men, Tiny, tend to become bombastic,'
'It doesn't suit you, my lovely, to be quite so sarcastic.'
Pass the port round again, drop the napkins on the floor,
On all quietness and grace let us close the door,
Let us stick to our own opinions and shout down the others,
The something something sons and daughters of their mothers.
WheeEEE . . . goes the bus starting up from bottom into second,
And as though Death itself, with an alabaster hand, beckoned,
Silence falls. Foes look quickly into the eyes of friends,
Seeking with gentle glance to make amends,
While the quarrelling hearts rush lovingly to each other in fear . . .
Is it the end of the Warning or the start of the All Clear?

Every hostess likes to plan something new and original in the form of table decoration, but not one has, I think, equalled the achievement of Mrs ——, whose guests at a recent party sat down to a table the centre-piece of which consisted of a pond in which were twenty live ducklings, small and fluffy and, apparently, not at all unhappy at being surrounded by strangers.   *(Evening Standard)*

from The Needle's Eye

Margaret Drabble

'How unlike Rose to be so late,' said Diana . . . and it was evident, immediately, from the tone in which these words were spoken, that Rose was the honoured guest, the star, the sanction for the evening's gathering, and that her presence, thus transformed into absence, was threatening to turn itself into as great an embarrassment as her arrival would have been a triumph. 'I can't think what can have happened, should I give her a ring, Nick?'

'I don't know,' said Nick, who was helping himself to another drink, reluctant to allow his wife's anxiety to spread, but not quite sure, because himself anxious, of how he could contain it. 'Let's give her another five minutes, should we?'

'All right,' said Diana, brightly, thinking with panic of the cassoulet slowly drying, the salad slowly crumpling into its dressing, and, worst horror, the mousse beginning to sink. She was never very sure about mousse, it was usually all right but she didn't trust it, nor did she trust herself not to have another drink, out of desperation, and if she did she knew that she would probably start dropping things in the kitchen and burning her hands when she got things out of the oven. One disastrous dinner-party, just before Nick had left her, she had dropped the lid of the iron casserole on her foot, under the influence of a whisky too many, an accident which had proved amazingly painful, and which had in fact precipitated his departure, because when the guests had gone she had accused him of never helping to carry anything, and they had had a dreadful row, because he had said that when he did carry things she got equally angry with him for not staying and amusing their guests. She couldn't decide, either, and was becoming increasingly incapable of deciding whether she ought to go and start warming up the soup now, or whether that would ruin the soup too, and moreover make it too clear to Rose, when she did come, if she did come, that she was very late. On the whole she much preferred people not to realise that they were late because it upset her so much when they had to apologise. She ate an olive and tried to sit still. Nick, meanwhile, was embarking on the subject of Rose: she wished he wouldn't, because if Rose didn't come it would make them look so silly, like boasting that one had invited the Queen but unfortunately she hadn't been able to come.

50

A Company of Friends

Elizabeth Jennings

Elizabeth Jennings.

We were all friends that night and sitting round
A lateish dinner. Candles lit us and
Shyness disappeared. Some golden ground
Surely held us. We could understand
Love's mishaps, teenage children and the sound
    Of their troubles. Here,

Close to a river and a city where
Learning's been current long, you could accept
Its implications. Last night we could share
The worth of art and promises well kept
Until that hour. Here was a world of care
    And I think we all slept

51

Better for our words of joy and grief.
We ate, we drank, ideas seemed to come
So easily. Here was abundant life
And grace shone like a happy coming home.
We did not notice that the time was brief
　　As every candle flame.

We gave time back to one another as
We shook warm hands and called a clear Good Night.
Now it's last night's tomorrow and I pass
That feast like film before my eyes and light
My long room with that silver and that glass
　　And glory in the sight.

Glass

Alan Pryce-Jones

The hospitality of glass cannot be exaggerated. Indeed, without glass a great many sensuous pleasures would not exist for us. Where would colored drinks be without glass to contain them? I cannot imagine a marble urn of crème de menthe, or a porcelain claret bottle. Indeed, it is to the condition of glass that other containers aspire. We like our china paperthin, so that the light streams through it; we prefer our urns of alabaster. But none of these materials react with such sparkle as glass to the exterior world. Not only does it allow the claret to glow through from within, but it steals light from the sun whenever it can. Give it a facet, or even a curve, and it will wink back at you with the manifold refraction of a prism.

Nothing about a house gives so keen a sense of hospitality. This is partly because glass is a gay substance. We speak, not without reason, of crystal laughter; and we link the glitter of a chandelier with comfortable-sounding objects like goblets and tumblers. The transparency helps. After all, we like seeing through our friends as well as catching a sudden reflection of their brightness. And so the presence of glasses in a room at once gives it a party air.

Johnnie! Me and You

Corney Grain

Oh! Johnnie! 'ere's a dinner party
   Look at all them things!
Oh! look at all them dishes
   Wot that powder'd footman brings!
Well, if they eat all that there food
   'Ow poorly they will be!
'Ere jump upon my back Johnnie!
   Now then you can see!
Oh! Johnnie! look at that ole gent,
   They've took 'is plate away!
Afore 'e's finished 'arf 'is food,
   That is a game to play!

No! that ain't beer they're drinkin' of
   Not likely, why that's fizz!
Oh! look at that great pink thing there,
   That's salmon fish, that is!
I think there's some mistake 'ere Johnnie!
   We ain't arst tonight!
We could a-pick'd a bit, eh Johnnie?
   We've got the appetite!
Seein' all that food there
   Makes yer 'ungry, that it do!
We ain't 'ad no dinner-parties lately,
   Johnnie! me and you!

Oh! Johnnie! look at that old gal,
   With only 'arf a gown,
That h'ice she's swaller'd must 'ave cost,
   Ah! well night 'arf a crown.
She's 'avin 'arf a quartern now,
   And wants it, that she do,

When I've eaten too much h'ice myself,
   I've 'ad that feelin' too!
Oh! Johnnie! they've pulled down the blind,
   I call it nasty mean.
They're all ashamed that's wot they is,
   Ashamed o' bein' seen
A-eatin' all that food like that,
'Tain't decent, that it 'ain't!
We wouldn't pull no blinds down
   If we'd 'arf o' their complaint!
So come along, let's orf it, Johnnie,
   Orf it to the Strand,
Now don't yer go a-cryin' Johnnie,
   'Ere give me your 'and.
'Ungry, Johnnie, so am I.
   We'll get a brown or two
A-callin' 'Keb or Kerridge, Captin'!'
   Johnnie! me and you!

from An Ideal Husband

Oscar Wilde

*The play opens in the octagon room of Sir Robert and Lady Chiltern's house
in Grosvenor Square, London. After dinner, 1895.*

Mrs Marchmont *and* Lady Basildon, *two very pretty women,
are seated together on a Louis Seize sofa. They are types of
exquisite fragility. Their affectation of manner has a delicate
charm. Watteau would have loved to paint them.*
MRS MARCHMONT: Going on to the Hartlocks' to-night,
Margaret?

LADY BASILDON: I suppose so. Are you?

MRS MARCHMONT: Yes. Horribly tedious parties they give, don't they?

LADY BASILDON: Horribly tedious! Never know why I go. Never know why I go anywhere.

MRS MARCHMONT: I come here to be educated.

LADY BASILDON: Ah! I hate being educated!

MRS MARCHMONT: So do I. It puts one almost on a level with the commercial classes, doesn't it? But dear Gertrude Chiltern is always telling me that I should have some serious purpose in life. So I come here to try and find one.

LADY BASILDON (*looking round through her lorgnette*): I don't see anybody here to-night whom one could possibly call a serious purpose. The man who took me in to dinner talked to me about his wife the whole time.

MRS MARCHMONT: How very trivial of him!

LADY BASILDON: Terribly trivial! What did your man talk about?

MRS MARCHMONT: About myself.

LADY BASILDON (*languidly*): And were you interested?

MRS MARCHMONT: (*shaking her head*): Not in the smallest degree.

LADY BASILDON: What martyrs we are, dear Margaret!

MRS MARCHMONT (*rising*): And how well it becomes us, Olivia!

They rise and go towards the music-room.

I Could Have Danced All Night

On with the dance! Let joy be unconfined!
No sleep till morn, when Youth and Pleasure meet
To chase the glowing hours with flying feet.

Byron, *Childe Harold's Pilgrimage*

from John Halifax, Gentleman
Mrs Craik

Dancing began. Spite of my Quaker education, or perhaps for that very reason, I delighted to see dancing. Dancing, such as it was then, when young folk moved breezily and lightly, as if they loved it; skimming like swallows down the long lines of the Triumph – gracefully winding in and out through the graceful country dance – lively always, but always decorous. In those days people did not think it necessary to the pleasures of dancing that any stranger would have liberty to snatch a shy, innocent girl round the waist, and whirl her about in mad waltz or awkward polka, till she stops, giddy and breathless, with burning cheek and tossed hair, looking – as I would not have liked to see our pretty Maud look. No; though while watching the little lady to-night, I was inclined to say to her –

> 'When you do dance, I wish you
> A wave o' the sea, that you might ever do
> Nothing but that.'

And in her unwearied spirits she seemed as if she would readily have responded to the wish.

from Queen Victoria's Diary

Friday, 24th May 1833 – To-day is my birthday. I am today fourteen years old! How VERY OLD! . . . At a ¼ to 6 we dined. At ½ past 7 we went with Charles, the Duchess of Northumberland, Lady Catherine Jenkinson, Lehzen, Sir George Anson, and Sir John, to a Juvenile Ball that was given in honour of my birthday at St James's by the King and Queen. We went into the Closet. Soon after the doors were opened, and the King leading

me went into the ball-room. Madame Bourdin was there as dancing-mistress. Victoire was also there, as well as MANY other children whom I knew. Dancing began soon after. I danced first with my cousin, George Cambridge, then with Prince George Lieven, then with Lord Brook, then March, then with Lord Athlone, then with Lord Fitzroy Lennox, then with Lord Emlyn. We then went to supper. It was ½ past 11; the King leading me again. I sat between the King and Queen. We left supper soon. My health was drunk. I then danced one more quadrille with Lord Paget. I danced in all 8 quadrilles. We came home at half-past 12. I was VERY much amused.

> Since the opening of the season women, stockingless and wearing their toe-nails painted to match their sandals and dresses, have been noticed on the floors of some of the leading public ballrooms. The vogue of the painted toe-nail has arrived at last. Scarlet nails really look quite aesthetic when worn with pale blue sandals and a light dress. The plain painted nails cost five shillings, and each coating needs renewing once a fortnight.
>
> *(Daily Express)*

from Emily Shore's Journal

aged 14½ years

WOODBURY, JUNE 23 1834

There was a tea-party at the Astells', during which I contrived to keep close to Miss Caroline, and had a great deal of merry conversation with her, of which the following is a sample:

Emily. I have a question to ask you. At balls and such places, what do people talk about? If they talk about neither sciences nor natural history, I shall set them down as thoroughly stupid.

Miss Car. Stupid! Oh dear me! let me see – they talk about neither sciences nor natural history.

Em. Stupid people! What do they talk about?

Miss Car. About? Oh, music.

Em. Music?

What is more beautiful for the blonde to wear for formal dances than white tulle? My answer—and I'm sure you will agree with me—is 'Nothing'.

Worcester (Massachusetts) Evening Gazette

Miss Car. Yes, music.

Em. Well, music's allowable – very proper. What else?

Miss Car. Yes, they talk about music, and how hot the last party was, and which they shall go to next; and they talk scandal, and on the works of the day.

Em. Dear me! what foolish people! to talk about such absurd things! And do you really like to go to such places, Miss Caroline? Do you actually like it?

Miss Car. Yes, very much indeed (! ! !).

Em. Like it! How horrid! How can you like it? What a very great waste of your time, when you ought to be learning and improving your mind, to go to balls and talk nothing but nonsense! Where is the pleasure of it? Do you not think it a waste of time?

Miss Car. Yes, I confess it is; it is a corrupt habit, but when once you have got it, you can never get rid of it.

Em. That is horrible to think of. I hope I shall never get it! But if amusement is your object, why don't you study natural history? There's no amusement so great as that.

Miss Car. But I confess that I don't like natural history.

Em. Oh, how very wrong! You ought to like it.

Miss Car. But nobody taught me; when I was a child nobody took pains with me.

Em. Very true; then it is not so much your fault. But now, may I ask you, Miss Caroline, when you once begin in the season to go to parties, at what rate do you go? how many a week?

Miss Car. Oh, why – sometimes to three in a night.

Em. Three in one night! What a waste of life!

from Her First Ball

Katherine Mansfield

Dark girls, fair girls were patting their hair, tying ribbons again, tucking handkerchiefs down the front of their bodices, smoothing marble-white gloves. And because they were all laughing it seemed to Leila that they were all lovely.

'Aren't there any invisible hair-pins?' cried a voice. 'How most extraordinary! I can't see a single invisible hair-pin.'

'Powder my back, there's a darling,' cried some one else.

'But I must have a needle and cotton. I've torn simply miles and miles of the frill,' wailed a third.

Then, 'Pass them along, pass them along!' The straw basket of programmes was tossed from arm to arm. Darling little pink-and-silver programmes, with pink pencils and fluffy tassels. Leila's fingers shook as she took one out of the basket. She wanted to ask some one, 'Am I meant to have one too?' but she had just time to read: 'Waltz 3. *Two, Two in a Canoe*. Polka 4. *Making the Feathers Fly*,' when Meg cried, 'Ready, Leila?' and they pressed their way through the crush in the passage towards the big double doors of the drill hall.

Dancing had not begun yet, but the band had stopped tuning, and the noise was so great it seemed that when it did begin to play it would never be heard. Leila, pressing close to Meg, looking over Meg's shoulder, felt that even the little quivering coloured flags strung across the ceiling were talking. She quite forgot to be shy; she forgot how in the middle of dressing she had sat down on the bed with one shoe off and one shoe on and begged her mother to ring up her cousins and say she couldn't go after all. And the rush of longing she had had to be sitting on the verandah of their forsaken up-country home, listening to the baby owls crying 'More pork' in the moonlight, was changed to a rush of joy so sweet that it was hard to bear alone. She clutched her fan, and, gazing at the gleaming, golden floor, the azaleas, the lanterns, the stage at one end with its red carpet and gilt chairs and the band in a corner, she thought breathlessly, 'How heavenly; how simply heavenly!'

from Hints on Etiquette

Do not wear *black* or coloured gloves, lest your partner look sulky; even should you be in *mourning*, wear *white* gloves, *not black*. People in DEEP *mourning* have no business in a ballroom at all.

LEAD the lady through the quadrille; do not *drag* her, nor clasp her hands as if it were made of wood, lest she not unjustly think you a boor.

You will not, if you are wise, stand up in a quadrille without knowing something of the figure; and if you are master of a few of the steps, *so much the better*. But dance quietly; do not kick and caper about, nor sway your body to and fro: dance only *from the hips downwards*; and lead the lady as lightly as you would tread a measure with a spirit of gossamer.

Dancing, 8 Spring Gardens

Lady Charlotte Guest

Lady Charlotte Guest was presented at Court, to William IV, in 1831.
She did not enjoy social life or dancing and said:

I always feel so solitary at all the gay things.
I fear I aquitted myself very ill.

This rhyme expresses her feelings: that most balls were stupid!

Oh dancing is the bane of my whole life
It gives me jealous pain and envy rife
When I go round and round so does the room!
I sit down on the ground, my usual doom!
I can't quadrille or 'lance', I can't 'cotill'
I can't dance any dance they make me ill.
I cannot 'Polk' or valse, I'm fat and slow!
But supper never palls, that's why I go.

......*dance only from the hips downwards*.......

Amongst My Friends

Colin West

Amongst my friends
I number some
Sixteen or so
Who dance.
Some like to do
The rhumba, some
Will waltz if they've
The chance;
And even in their slumber, some
Will foxtrot in
A trance.
But as for me,
I'm cumbersome,
And all I do
Is prance.

> Lady Veronica wore toe-less black sandals, but had not, I noticed, adopted the fashion for toed stockings. Hers, however, were sufficiently transparent to afford those who cared to see them glimpses of nails enamelled red.   *(Evening Standard)*

from The Ugly One

Hermione, Countess of Ranfurly

As we grew older, embarrassments were frequent. Leaving a very stately home after a lovely weekend, I watched my absent-minded sister, Cynthia, pressing her small tip into the hand of our millionaire host and kissing the butler goodbye. On another occasion, at a ball, a soiled sanitary towel suddenly appeared on the dance floor. At first few noticed it but after a while, as it was shifted around the floor by long, swirling skirts, it became the centre of attention. Our partners steered us carefully round it but, when the music stopped and we all sat down, it remained resplendent on the centre of the dance floor. At last, after what seemed an eternity, a blushing footman carrying a silver salver and sugar tongs removed it, to great applause.

Sometimes, by mistake, we arrived at parties to which we'd not been invited. This was easy to do because dances were going on in London in every direction – often in the same hotel or area. On one dreadful evening when I arrived innocently and cheerfully at the wrong party, a furious host picked me up and flung me out on to the street, ruining my dress and hair-do, and grazing my face. Not long afterwards, when I was married to Dan and we gave a party, he appeared and we had the satisfaction of asking him to leave as he had not been invited.

from A Christmas Carol

Charles Dickens

There were more dances, and there were forfeits, and more dances, and there was cake, and there was negus, and there was a great piece of Cold Roast, and there was a great piece of Cold Boiled, and there were mince-pies, and plenty of beer. But the great effect of the evening came after the Roast and Boiled, when the fiddler (an artful dog, mind! The sort of man who knew his business better than you or I could have told it him!) struck up 'Sir Roger de Coverley'. Then old Fezziwig stood out to dance with Mrs Fezziwig. Top couple too; with a good stiff piece of work cut out for them; three or four and twenty pair of partners; people who were not to be trifled with; people who *would* dance, and had no notion of walking.

But if they had been twice as many: ah, four times: old Fezziwig would have been a match for them, and so would Mrs Fezziwig. As to *her*, she was worthy to be his partner in every sense of the term. If that's not high praise, tell me higher, and I'll use it. A positive light appeared to issue from Fezziwig's calves. They shone in every part of the dance like moons. You couldn't have predicted, at any given time, what would become of 'em next. And when old Fezziwig and Mrs Fezziwig had gone all through the dance; advance and retire, hold hands with your partner; bow and curtsey; corkscrew; thread-the-needle, and back again to your place; Fezziwig 'cut' – cut so deftly, that he appeared to wink with his legs, and came upon his feet again without a stagger.

When the clock struck eleven, this domestic ball broke up. Mr and Mrs Fezziwig took their stations, one on either side the door, and shaking hands with every person individually as he or she went out, wished him or her a Merry Christmas.

from Best Behaviour

Mary Killen

Dress Tucked into Tights

Q. What is the correct protocol for alerting someone that they have been dancing reels for a full fifteen minutes with their dress tucked into their tights at the back? The incident I witnessed occurred at the Northern Meeting and involved a rather formidable fifty-year-old local dignitary of my acquaintance who had just emerged from the ladies cloakroom before taking the floor and was obviously slightly the worse for wear. Although the spectacle was exceedingly enjoyable to watch, I felt it was rather *lese majeste* and that I, or someone, should have done something. Yet, as you can imagine, no one could bring themselves to tell her. What should we have done?

A.St C., The Black Isle

A. *As many of those men present would have undoubtedly been wearing skean-dhus, it should have been relatively easy for one of them to put his dagger-like instrument to effective use by discreetly slashing the elastic at the waistband of the tights worn by the lady in question while engaging her in seated conversation. In this way the skirts of the dress would have been swiftly returned to floor level.*

How should one best alert someone who has been dancing reels for fifteen minutes that their skirt is tucked into their tights?

For the evening, long suede or kid gloves if you like. It is a fashion to carry them and drop them about for someone to pick up.

(Woman's Journal)

I've Danced with a Man Who's Danced with a Girl

Herbert Farjeon

My word, I've had a party,
My word, I've had a spree,
Believe me or believe me not,
It's all the same to me!
I'm wild with exultation,
I'm dizzy with success,
For I've danced with a man,
I've danced with a man
Who – well, you'll never guess.

I've danced with a man who's danced with a girl
Who's danced with the Prince of Wales!
I'm crazy with excitement!
Completely off the rails!
And when *he* said to me what *she* said to him
The Prince remarked to her,
He held my hand –
It was simply grand –
And I made no demur!

Glory, glory, hallelujah!
I'm the luckiest of females!
For I've danced with a man
Who's danced with a girl
Who's danced with the Prince of Wales!

It's true my partner's dancing
Would not have won a prize,
He couldn't do the Charleston
Though he had several tries.
His tango was the limit,
His waltzing much too stiff,
But suchlike little blemishes
Seem unimportant IF

You dance with a man who's danced with a girl
Who's danced with the Prince of Wales!
It's the Great Big Thing that matters –
A fig for the mere details!
And when *he* said to me what *she* said to him
The Prince remarked to her,
We were standing right
In the bright moonlight,
And I made no demur!
Glory, glory, hallelujah!
I'm the luckiest of females!
For I've danced with a man
Who's danced with a girl
Who's danced with the Prince of Wales!

from The Old Century

Siegfried Sassoon

There is no need to be exact about the date, but it is somewhere in the early part of June 1906, and about five o'clock in the morning. In broad daylight, under a quietly overclouded sky, a dozen young people are arranging themselves before the canopied fountain in the market-place at Cambridge. They have danced to the end of the Trinity Boat Club Ball and are about to corroborate the occasion by being photographed.

They are doing it in a good-natured unresisting sort of way, for it is a family party and they all take one another's presence as a matter of course, without any nonsense about wondering when they will meet again.

After the Trinity Boat Club Ball, Cambridge, June 1906.
Siegfried Sassoon is seated centre, on the ground.

My cousin Alyce stifles a yawn and feels sure that the camera will catch her in the middle of the next one; my cousin Joan tells her brother Oliver to put his tie straight; the photographer emerges from black velvet obscurity, regards the group with a stabilizing simper, and removes the cap; for three seconds time holds its breath, and then relaxes us into animation again. A clock strikes five and the young people disappear in various directions, unaware that I shall have my eye on them more than thirty years afterwards. Scrutinizing that faded photograph now, I see myself surrounded by my cousins – the girls looking absentmindedly amused and the men rather stolid and serious. There is that modest hero Malcolm, a stalwart Rowing Blue, destined to become an eminent surgeon. And his younger brother, who went into the Indian Army. And Oliver, who was to do well as an engineer. And my brother Hamo, whose engineering ambitions were sacrificed on the Gallipoli peninsula. And there am I, sitting on the ground in front, with a serenely vacant countenance which suggests that no plans for a practical career have as yet entered my head. Behind that head the jet of the drinking-fountain is just visible, as though the camera were hinting that my name would be written in water, which was what I myself sometimes foresaw.

It had been a jolly fine dance anyhow, I thought, picking up my cap and gown and taking my tired patent-leather feet across to my rooms, which were only about fifty yards from the fountain.

May Ball

Roger McGough

The evening lay before us
like her silken dress
arranged carefully over the bed.
It would be a night to remember.
We would speak of it often
in years to come. There would
be good food and wine,
cabaret, and music to dance to.
How we'd dance.
How we'd laugh.
We would kiss indiscreetly,
and what are lawns for
but to run barefoot across?

But the evening didn't do
what it was told.
It's the morning after now
and morningafter cold.
I don't know what went wrong
but I blame her. After all
I bought the tickets.
Of course, I make no mention,
that's not my style,
and I'll continue to write
at least for a while.
I carry her suitcase down to the hall,
our first (and her last) University Ball.

"I thought we might want to slip away early"

from Goodnight to the Season

Winthrop Mackworth Praed

Goodnight to the Season! the dances,
   The fillings of hot little rooms,
The glancings of rapturous glances,
   The fancyings of fancy costumes.
The pleasures which Fashion makes duties,
   The praisings of fiddles and flutes,
The luxury of looking at beauties,
   The tedium of talking to mutes;
The female diplomatists, planners
   Of matches for Laura and Jane,
The ice of her Ladyship's manners,
   The ice of his Lordship's champagne.

Goodnight to the Season! another
   Will come with its trifles and toys,
And hurry away like its brother,
   In sunshine, and odour, and noise.
Will it come with a rose or a briar?
   Will it come with a blessing or curse?
Will its bonnets be lower or higher?
   Will its morals be better or worse?
Will it find me grown thinner or fatter,
   Or fonder of wrong or of right,
Or married, – or buried? – no matter,
   Goodnight to the season, Good-night!

After the ball is over, after the break of morn,
After the dancers leaving, after the stars are gone;
Many a heart is aching if you could read them all,
Many the hopes that have vanished, after the ball.

(Charles K. Harris)

A LOT OF PARTIES

The Greshams' party was, after all, not quite like other parties, for they had lamas at it, fresh from Tibet . . . it made the party quite distinctive and everyone enjoyed it very much.

Rose Macaulay, Crewe Train

I've Been to a Marvellous Party

Noël Coward

Verse 1   Quite for no reason
I'm here for the Season
And high as a kite,
Living in error
With Maud at Cap Ferrat
Which couldn't be right.
Everyone's here and frightfully gay,
Nobody cares what people say,
Though the Riviera
Seems really much queerer
Than Rome at its height,
Yesterday night –

Refrain 1 I've been to a marvellous party
With Nounou and Nada and Nell,
It was in the fresh air
And we went as we were
And we stayed as we were
Which was Hell.
Poor Grace started singing at midnight
And didn't stop singing till four;
We knew the excitement was bound to begin
When Laura got blind on Dubonnet and gin
And scratched her veneer with a Cartier pin,
I couldn't have liked it more.

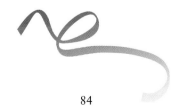

Refrain 2 I've been to a marvellous party,
            I must say the fun was intense,
            We all had to do
            What the people we knew
            Would be doing a hundred years hence.
            Dear Cecil arrived wearing armour,
            Some shells and a black feather boa,
            Poor Millicent wore a surrealist comb
            Made of bits of mosaic from St Peter's in Rome,
            But the weight was so great that she had to go
                home,
            I couldn't have liked it more!

Verse 2   People's behaviour
            Away from Belgravia
            Would make you aghast,
            So much variety

Watching Society
Scampering past,
If you have any mind at all
Gibbon's divine *Decline and Fall*
Seems pretty flimsy,
No more than a whimsy,
By way of contrast
On Saturday last –

Refrain 3 I've been to a marvellous party,
We didn't start dinner till ten
And young Bobbie Carr
Did a stunt at the bar
With a lot of extraordinary men;
Dear Baba arrived with a turtle
Which shattered us all to the core,
The Grand Duke was dancing a foxtrot with me
When suddenly Cyril screamed Fiddledidee
And ripped off his trousers and jumped in the sea,
I couldn't have liked it more.

Refrain 4 I've been to a marvellous party,
Elise made an entrance with May,
You'd never have guessed
From her fisherman's vest
That her bust had been whittled away.
Poor Lulu got fried on Chianti
And talked about esprit de corps.
Maurice made a couple of passes at Gus
And Freddie, who hates any kind of a fuss,
Did half the Big Apple and twisted his truss,
I couldn't have liked it more.

Refrain 5 I've been to a marvellous party,
We played the most wonderful game,
Maureen disappeared
And came back in a beard
And we all had to guess at her name!
We talked about growing old gracefully
And Elsie who's seventy-four
Said, 'A, it's a question of being sincere,
And B, if you're supple you've nothing to fear.'
Then she swung upside down from a glass
chandelier,
I couldn't have liked it more.

from Vile Bodies

Evelyn Waugh

'Oh, Nina, *what a lot of parties.*'

(. . . Masked parties, Savage parties, Victorian parties, Greek parties, Wild West parties, Russian parties, Circus parties, parties where one had to dress as somebody else, almost naked parties in St John's Wood, parties in flats and studios and houses and ships and hotels and night clubs, in windmills and swimming-baths, tea parties at school where one ate muffins and meringues and tinned crab, parties at Oxford where one drank brown sherry and smoked Turkish cigarettes, dull dances in London and comic dances in Scotland and disgusting dances in Paris – all that succession and repetition of massed humanity. . . . Those vile bodies . . .)

Sir Tom and Lady Cynthia Mosley proved that at their very successful party down at Wincanton. . . . It would be difficult to imagine any gathering more gifted with beauty and brains. Yet I fancy that the chief success of the evening was achieved by the simple process of throwing custard pies. Or, rather, éclairs. One fair lady caught one full in the eye.

(*The Tatler*)

Office Party

Alan Brownjohn

We were throwing out small-talk
On the smoke-weary air,
When the girl with the squeaker
Came passing each chair.

She was wearing a white dress,
Her paper-hat was a blue
Crown with a red tassel,
And to every man who

Glanced up at her, she leant over
And blew down the hole,
So the squeaker inflated
And began to unroll.

She stopped them all talking
With this trickery,
And she didn't leave out anyone
Until she came to me.

I looked up and she met me
With a half-teasing eye
And she took a mild breath and
Went carefully by.

And with cold concentration
To the next man she went,
And squawked out the instrument
To its fullest extent.

And whether she passed me
Thinking that it would show
Too much favour to mock me
I never did know –

Or whether her withholding
Was her cruelty,
And it was that she despised me,
I couldn't quite see –

So it could have been discretion,
And it could have been disgust,
But it was quite unequivocal,
And suffer it I must:

All I know was: she passed me,
Which I did not expect
– And I'd never so craved for
Some crude disrespect.

from Bridget Jones's Diary

Helen Fielding

MONDAY 17 APRIL

8st 12, alcohol units 0 (v.g.), cigarettes 0 (v.g.), Instants 5 (but won £2 so total instants expenditure only £3).

Right. Tomorrow is *Kafka's Motorbike*. Am going to work out clear set of objectives. In a minute. Will just watch adverts then ring up Jude.

Right

1) Not to get too pissed.
2) To aim to meet people to network with.
Hmmm. Anyway, will think of some more later.

11 p.m. Right.

3) To put the social skills from the article into action.
4) ~~To make Daniel think I have inner poise and want to get off with me again. No. No.~~
4) ~~To meet and sleep with sex god.~~

4) To make interesting contacts in the publishing world, possibly even other professions in order to find new career.

Oh God. Do not want to go to scary party. Want to stay home with bottle of wine and watch *Eastenders*.

TUESDAY 18 APRIL

9st 0, alcohol units 7 (oh dear), cigarettes 30, calories (cannot bear to think about it), Instants 1 (excellent).

Party got off to a bad start when could not see anyone that I knew to introduce to each other. Found myself a drink then spotted Perpetua talking to James from the *Telegraph*. Approached Perpetua confidently, ready to swing into action but instead of saying 'James, Bridget comes from Northamptonshire and is a keen gymnast' (am going to start going to gym again soon), Perpetua just carried on talking – well beyond the two-minute mark – and ignored me.

I hung around for a while feeling a total git, then spotted Simon from Marketing. Cunningly pretending I had not intended to join Perpetua's conversation at all, I bore down purposefully upon Simon, preparing to say, 'Simon Barnett!' in the style of Tina Brown. When I was almost there, however, I noticed that, unfortunately, Simon from Marketing was talking to Julian Barnes. Suspecting that I might not be able to fully pull off crying, 'Simon Barnett! Julian Barnes!' with quite the required gaiety and *tone*, I hovered indecisively then started to sidle away, at which point Simon said in an irritated superior voice (one you, funnily enough, never hear him use when he is trying to get off with you by the photocopier), 'Did you want something, Bridget?'

'Ah! Yes!' I said, panicking wildly about what it was I could possibly want. 'Ahm.'

'Yeees?' Simon and Julian Barnes looked at me expectantly.

'Do you know where the toilets are?' I blurted. Damn. Damn. Why? Why did I say that? I saw a faint smile hover over the thin-but-attractive lips of Julian Barnes.

'Ah, actually I think they're over there. Jolly good. Thanks,' I said, and made for the exit. Once out of the swing doors I slumped against the wall, trying to get my breath back, thinking, 'inner poise, inner poise'. It was not going particularly well so far, there were no two ways about it.

I looked wistfully at the stairs. The thought of going home, putting my nighty on and turning on the telly began to seem irresistibly attractive. Remembering the Party Objectives, though, I breathed in deeply through my nose, murmured, 'inner poise' and pushed through the doors back into the party.

Doing it in style.
Cover for the Oldie, *September 2003. Bob Wilson.*

Nel Mezzo Del Cammin*

John Mole

One old bean to another
At a Literary party: *I saw you*
In the pub before we got here
And said to myself that's an old bean
I recognise but don't recall
His name. Remind me. Yes
Of course you are. I thought
We were both dead. Delighted.

And you? The pair of them
Have turned to me. I tell them
I'm a middling bean, past fifty
But not much. They raise their glasses
Here's to youth! And what do
You write? Poetry, I tell them.
Jolly good, they say, *Delighted.*
*Do you rhyme? Who **are** you?*

So the party goes, so many glasses
Raised to this and that, to faces
Glimpsed across the room, then
Home. A nightcap as my son
Comes last thing from a pub
Where all the young beans gather
Knowing everyone. *Enjoy yourself?*
We ask each other. *Jolly good!*

*In the middle of the road of our life.

from Not Another Little Sod

Simon Brett

Little Sod faces his third year with every intention of continuing to make his parents' life hell . . .

TWENTY-FIFTH MONTH

Give them their due, though, they do sometimes make an effort. Today, for instance, they arranged a birthday party for me. Both took the afternoon off work, which is quite something. They'd really pushed the boat out – lots of cakes, jellies, crisps, etc. And a great pile of sweetie-bags for me.

Great, I thought. Finally my parents are giving me the lifestyle I deserve.

Then they went and spoiled it all by inviting a whole bunch of other toddlers to share the goodies! They even invited the most despised object in the world – Baby Einstein, who was born round the same time as me and has since then driven me mad by making every developmental advance months before I've even thought about it.

At least I saw to it today that Baby Einstein went home wiping cream and jelly out of tear-stained eyes.

But the worst thing was – my parents gave the sweetie-bags away to all the other toddlers! I was only left with one! Talk about mean.

Next time I have a birthday party, I'll choose the guest list. And there won't be anyone else on it.

On the other hand, I do get more presents this way. All the guest toddlers brought me something.

By the way, at the end of last year, my parents came up with what I can only assume was their idea of a joke: they pretended they were going to have another baby. I'm glad to say I haven't heard any more of that nonsense since. There is no New Baby on the way.

DAY 2

They've got a nerve! I would have thought my behaviour yesterday had made my views on the subject absolutely clear, and yet this afternoon I'm packed off to Baby Einstein's birthday party! (Not only always more advanced than me, the little creep is also a day younger.)

Still, the same ammunition was to hand, so I saw to it that Baby Einstein ended a second party wiping cream and jelly out of tear-stained eyes.

My dad left work early to pick me up. I was given a sweetie-bag as I was leaving and He said jokingly to my hostess, 'Maybe I should take another one for the New Baby when it arrives . . . ?'

If they want to keep going on about the New Baby, I suppose that's up to them. I don't care. I got two sweetie-bags out of it.

Party

Joyce Grenfell

Oh Arthur, they're coming!
The party's begun –
How d'you do, Miss Montgomery,
Hello, Mr Dunn.
D'you know Major Wimble,
Sir Christopher Cook?
What fun, darling Dorothy,

How lovely you look!
Sir Wincanton Pluggley,
Mrs Borridge. (Oh hell –
Oh Arthur, Cousin Caroline's
Turned up as well.)
Mrs Mostyn and Mavis,
The Vicar, John Drew.
Hello, Cousin Caroline!
How nice to see you.

So glad you could come
How good of you to spare
The time
For it's just
An informal affair.

Hello, Colonel Saxby,
Miss Bell, Mr Stone.
(Arthur, look – Cousin Caroline's
Dancing alone!)

How nice, Lady Bley,
Professor Crumb Teazle,
And how is Bombay?
Oh here's Mrs Buzbee
And Alderman Clews
(Arthur, now she is waltzing
Without any shoes.)
Mrs Biscuit, John Wilby.
(Don't look – near the door.
Oh Arthur, Cousin Caroline's
Full length on the floor.)

So glad you could come
How good of you to spare
The time
For it's just
An informal affair.

(I'm under control now,
Not making a fuss.
Let's pretend that she isn't Related to Us.)
Hello, Mrs Pomfret
And Councillor Brice
And Dr Smith Wellerby
And Matron – how nice.
(Oh heavens – a silence,
They're all in a ring.
Oh Arthur, Cousin Caroline
Is starting to sing!)

from Toast: The Story of a Boy's Hunger

Nigel Slater

BIRTHDAY CAKE

Today is my tenth birthday and no one has even mentioned a party yet. I guess they must be keeping it as a surprise. Last year's was one of the best days of my life. Mum said she couldn't cope with so many people any more so we held it at a big house on Coleway Road called the Pines. All the crocuses were out in the garden and because it was so close to Easter everyone gave me chocolate Easter eggs. I ended up with about thirty eggs, then Mum told me off because when the last person

Cakes & Biscuits

arrived I said 'Oh no, not another egg', and he looked really disappointed. She said something about being ungrateful.

The Pines had someone there to organise the party. There was lots of running around and screaming. Much more than we had been allowed to do at other kids' parties. The best bit was the birthday cake, even though Mum didn't make it herself. She said it was too much for her. It was a great cake covered in Smarties and candles. We all took slices of it home, wrapped in paper serviettes, though mine stuck to the paper and all the colour came out of the Smarties. I felt bad afterwards because Paul Griffith's dad gave some of the boys a lift home and David Brooks was sick in the back of his car. I can't remember what happened to all the chocolate eggs.

Margaret Thatcher was also fond of chocolate,

as this newspaper cutting shows:

I hope Margaret Hilda's book will throw some light on the Case of The Stolen Chocolate Biscuits Hidden in the Knickers. The incident occurred at a children's birthday party in Grantham 60 years ago but is still remembered. A tempting spread was prepared, but eventually, alas, it was going home time. A trickle of chocolate on one little girl's white sock prompted an investigation. And yes, she was found to have a cache of biscuits in her drawers. Margaret Thatcher knows all about this. She was that girl.

I Wish I Didn't Talk So Much at Parties

Phyllis McGinley

I wish at parties I could learn
To sit and listen.

I wish I didn't talk so much at parties.
It isn't that I want to hear
My voice assaulting every ear,
Uprising loud and firm and clear
   Above the cocktail clatter.
It's simply, once a door bell's rung,
(I've been like this since I was young)
Some madness overtakes my tongue
   And I begin to chatter.

Buffet, ball, banquet, quilting bee,
   Wherever conversation's flowing,
Why must I feel it falls on me
   To keep things going?
Though ladies cleverer than I
   Can loll in silence, soft and idle,
Whatever topic gallops by,
   I seize its bridle,
Hold forth on art, dissect the stage,
   Or babble like a kindergartener
On politics, till I enrage
   My dinner partner.
I wish I didn't talk so much at parties.
When hotly boil the arguments,

Ah! would I had the common sense
To sit demurely on the fence
    And let who will be vocal,
Instead of plunging in the fray
With my opinions on display
Till all the gentlemen edge away
    To catch an early local.

I wish I didn't talk so much
I wish I didn't talk so much
I wish I didn't talk so much
When I am at a party.

from Eat, Drink and Be Merry

Sylvia Lynd

'AND WAS IT A NICE PARTY?'

With her wide eyes scarcely higher than the level of the table, she sat and longed for things. She felt she wanted to taste all the deliciousness that she could see, but before she had left her own house she had promised to take what was offered her and say 'Thank you'; and some of the things she most wanted never came her way at all. She got bread and butter to begin with, and then brown bread and butter, which was worse, and then a queen cake. None of the pink and white biscuits, or even the sponge fingers, came near her, and once when the chocolate cakes were next door but one, a slim hand, with bright nails and many sparkling rings, pounced talon-like upon the plate and bore it away right out of her view. There was 'skin' in her milk too, and there was no spoon with which to fish it out. She sat still at last, with the dry, uneaten half of the queen cake on the plate before her, and it was with difficulty that she kept the tears from overflowing her eyes.

And now they were cutting the Christmas cake, such splendid slices, coated with white sugar from bottom to top. Then a grown-up voice said: 'Oh, those slices are *much* too big. They'll never get through those!' And they took the knife again and cut all the slices in halves horizontally, so that some were nearly all sugar and some had hardly any sugar at all. Then they handed them round. She watched them coming towards her down the table. Some of the children took the top pieces with all the sugar; a few took the lower pieces that had hardly any. She hoped and hoped that one of the top pieces would come to her; but the girl next to her took the sugary bit, and she felt she must take the bit without the sugar, and the plate passed on.

The Party

Enid Clay

Not one was witty, gaiety was rare,
They sprawled in heaps, with cushions on the floor;
While someone vamped the latest jazz-time air
Till he grew tired, as we did long before.

And in the corner, where the drinks were found,
The wines were sour, the bubbly very flat;
And you were lucky, if on hunting round,
You got your own, and not another's hat.

There the pale sandwich, very under-hammed,
And the sad sausage, wilted with anaemia:
And there they sat, the dirty and the damned,
Wrecked on the dull shore of a sham Bohemia.

The Proudies Entertain

Anthony Trollope

The sofa had certainly been so placed that those who were behind it found great difficulty in getting out; – there was but a narrow gangway, which one person could stop. This was a bad arrangement, and one which Bertie thought it might be well to improve.

'Take care, Madeline,' said he; and turning to the fat rector added, 'Just help me with a slight push.'

The rector's weight was resting on the sofa, and unwittingly lent all its impetus to accelerate and increase the motion which Bertie intentionally originated. The sofa rushed from its moorings, and ran half-way into the middle of the room. Mrs Proudie was standing with Mr Slope in front of the signora, and had been trying to be condescending and sociable; but she was not in the very best of tempers; for she found that, whenever she spoke to the lady, the lady replied by speaking to Mr Slope. Mr Slope was a favourite, no doubt; but Mrs Proudie had no idea of being less thought of than the chaplain. She was beginning to be stately, stiff, and offended when unfortunately the castor of the sofa caught itself in her lace train, and carried away there is no saying how much of her garniture. Gathers were heard to go, stitches to crack, plaits to fly open, flounces were seen to fall, and breadths to expose themselves; – a long ruin of rent lace disfigured the carpet, and still clung to the vile wheel on which the sofa moved. . . .

As Juno may have looked at Paris on Mount Ida, so did Mrs Proudie look on Ethelbert Stanhope when he pushed the leg of the sofa into her lace train.

Bertie, when he saw what he had done, rushed over to the sofa, and threw himself on one knee before the offended lady.

His object, doubtless, was to liberate the torn lace from the castor; but he looked as though he were imploring pardon from a goddess.

'Unhand it, sir!' said Mrs Proudie. From what scrap of dramatic poetry she had extracted the word cannot be said; but it must have rested on her memory, and now seemed opportunely dignified for the occasion.

'I'll fly to the looms of the fairies to repair the damage, if you'll only forgive me,' said Ethelbert, still on his knees.

'Unhand it, sir!' said Mrs Proudie, with redoubled emphasis, and all but furious wrath. This allusion to the fairies was a direct mockery, and intended to turn her into ridicule. So at least it seemed to her. 'Unhand it, sir!' she almost screamed.

'It's not me; it's the cursed sofa,' said Bertie, looking imploringly in her face, and holding up both his hands to show that he was not touching her belongings, but still remaining on his knees.

'Unhand it, sir!'

Hereupon the signora laughed; not loud, indeed, but yet audibly. And as the tigress bereft of her young will turn with equal anger on any within reach, so did Mrs Proudie turn upon her female guest.

'Madam!' she said – and it is beyond the power of prose to tell of the fire which flashed from her eyes.

The signora stared her full in the face for a moment, and then turning to her brother said playfully, 'Bertie, you idiot, get up.'

By this time the bishop, and Mr Slope, and her three daughters were around her, and had collected together the wide ruins of her magnificence. The girls fell into circular rank behind their mother, and thus following her and carrying out the fragments, they left the reception rooms in a manner not altogether devoid of dignity. Mrs Proudie had to retire and re-array herself.

Suburban hostess to host: 'The party's not going very well, John. I wish some gate-crashers would come along and liven things up.'

from Complete Guide to Gatecrashing
Nicholas Allan

*Nicholas Allan, expert in the art of gatecrashing, admits to the occasional
'bad crash'. At one exclusive shop-launch party he was questioned
by a suspicious official, who soon sent for back-up:*

'Could we see your invitation, sir?'

'My partner Sarah's got it. She's still trying to park the car, I think.'

It wasn't so much the tone of voice as the simple inarguable forefinger curl informing me to follow him off the premises that wounded me so much.

Fortunately, the guests on the two floors we had to descend were too drunk to notice my chaperoned departure. They might have even thought I was so important I needed an escort to ensure a rapid exit. This, however, didn't assuage my humiliation.

Sometimes, on the few occasions this has happened, I wonder if it's damaged professional pride that depresses me, or is it really the idea of not being wanted? Stepping out into the still sunlit street, I said,

'It'll be okay if we come back with the invitation, won't it?'

He nodded with total disbelief, making me feel worse.

The story has a surprising twist. Promising myself never to ever contemplate crashing a party again – more, to live my life virtuously, like I did at school; never to lie or take anything without paying for it, never allowing myself to even say something I don't genuinely mean – I caught a bus to Charing Cross, crossed the bridge, and dropped in on the Festival Hall for a pee. In the lower atrium, a private party was well underway.

Immediately, in a reflex action, I skipped down the stairs, took a glass of Australian red, and noticed a woman who smiled. She said,

'Are you a gatecrasher?'

'Hardly,' I smiled back, 'I'm in general charge of administration here.'

The party was an end of conference celebration for a corporate firm; she too had an administrative position and had helped organise this event. She confided, later, she hated her job and envied mine of working at the Festival Hall. She asked if there were any similar positions coming up, and insisted that I take her details. Her friendliness extended to fetching me another glass of wine, and a lift home.

As we left the party, both warmed by each other's fortuitous meeting, and stepped into the relaxing seats of her corporate Mercedes, I felt a renewal of faith, a trust in the human heart. Trust, honesty: isn't it that what it's really all about?

My Party

Norman Silver

The intrepid gang of five hunt the pavements
for my house, camouflaged as it is between

many houses. They stash cider handgrenades
on the garage roof under my father's eyes

before ringing the doorbell. Potplants curl
their roots in tight shoes, refusing to dance.

My parents huddle in their bedroom, peeping
through curtains but pretending unconcern.

The party starts with sofa-cushion football,
kung fu with the peanut-bowl, spin the bottle

with dumb-giggly forfeits, and spray painting
the ceiling with Pepsi. As the cider explodes,

the intrepids, moved by cortexripping rhythms,
try to practise their sumo dancing on females.

Potplants fold their aching leaves. A war
of marshmallows and Maltesers is followed

by a crisp potato hurricane leaving the dead
and dying chocolates to bleed sog and gunge

on a mock Axminster battlefield. A gaggle
of girls in black skirts with sham zips

incite their warriors by flaunting breasts
and ululating from the skirting boards.

The wild things rumpus. Boys with beaks
and headfeathers howl and bellow and bark,

duelling for supremacy with antlers clashing.
Midnight is chimed by the smashing of windows

and my parents swiftly abandon their vigil.
They dustpan the debris and tend the wounded.

'Parents showing up at a party! Yuuuugh!'
The gang of five in their wolf-suits steal out

into the night jungle where the slow music
cannot harm them. Lingering couples sway

on the dancefloor, trailing in spilled cider.
Potplants dance together. I am a year older.

Nocturne

A.P. Herbert

This party is rather a bore;
I shall go to such parties no more.
   Will somebody kind
   My overcoat find
And quietly show me the door?

I'm weary of standing about,
Making silly remarks in a shout;
   The sandwiches taste
   Of photograph-paste,
And now the white wine has run out?
   I shall go to bed early tonight,
   I'm feeling a little bit done;
   But I like the young lady in white,
   And it's only a quarter to one.

Oh, why do we gather in herds,
Like a lot of excitable birds,
   And chatter and bawl
   About nothing at all

Manners and modes: After a surfeit of 'V' and 'U' backs,
nothing less than a 'Y' will hold the attention.

In wholly inaudible words?
There are seventy women and men
In this room, and it holds about ten.
   You heard what I said?
   I am going to bed,
And it's merely a question of 'When?'
   I shall go to bed early tonight,
   I'm feeling a little bit blue;
   But I like the young lady in white,
   And it's only a quarter to two.

There are too many people who write,
They're most of them present tonight;
   And how I abhor
   The musical bore
Who has collared the charmer in white!

And as for this girl with a mane,
She gives me a positive pain!
  She talks of James Joyce
  In a bronchial voice,
And I don't want to see her again.
  But I do like the lady in white,
  And I wish she was married to me.
  I shall go to bed early tonight –
  Oh, dear, it's a quarter to three!

There are too many people who paint;
It's becoming a chronic complaint;
  They're all of them here,
  They've finished the beer,
And I think I am going to faint,
But I've met the young lady in white;
Our talk was exciting but slight:
  'Good evening,' she said,
  'I am going to bed;
So glad to have met you. Good-night!'
  Still, I've met the young lady in white,
  And I wish we had met a bit more.
  I shall go to bed early tonight –
  Oh, gosh! it's a quarter to four!

Advertisement for the London store Marshall & Snelgrove, 1914.

from Jonathan Strange & Mr Norrell

Susanna Clarke

And how to describe a London party? Candles in lustres of cut-glass are placed everywhere about the house in dazzling profusion; elegant mirrors triple and quadruple the light until night outshines day; many-coloured hothouse fruits are piled up in stately pyramids upon white-clothed tables, divine creatures, resplendent with jewels, go about the room in pairs, arm in arm, admired by all who see them. Yet the heat is over-powering, the pressure and noise almost as bad; there is nowhere to sit and scarce anywhere to stand. You may see your dearest friend in another part of the room; you may have a world of things to tell him – but how in the world will you ever reach him? If you are fortunate then perhaps you will discover him later in the crush and shake his hand as you are both hurried past each other. Surrounded by cross, hot strangers, your chance of rational conversation is equal to what it would be in an African desert. Your only wish is to preserve your favourite gown from the worst ravages of the crowd. Every body complains of the heat and the suffocation. Every body declares it to be entirely insufferable. But if it is all misery for the guests, then what of the wretchedness of those who have not been invited? Our sufferings are nothing to theirs! And we may tell each other tomorrow that it was a delightful party.

FUN AND GAMES

Guests *must* join in, even if they don't feel like it. If they all get together and try, presently from their midst up floats the frail ethereal spirit – Enjoyment. The party's going.

We may be very cheery on our upper halves, but underneath, do you not know there lies a profound melancholy which makes one above such things? It is best to think that this is not the soul's dissatisfaction with living, but merely liver, for the latter is easier to cure.

The Family Weekend Book

My Party

Kit Wright

My parents said I could have a party
And that's just what I did.

Dad said, 'Who had you thought of inviting?'
I told him. He said, 'Well, you'd better start writing,'
And that's just what I did.

To:
Phyllis Willis, Horace Morris,
Nancy, Clancy, Bert and Gert Sturt,
Dick and Mick and Nick Crick,
Ron, Don, John,
Dolly, Molly, Polly –
Neil Peel –
And my dear old friend, Dave Dirt.

I wrote, 'Come along, I'm having a party,'
And that's just what they did.

They all arrived with huge appetites
As Dad and I were fixing the lights.
I said, 'Help yourself to the drinks and bites!'
And that's just what they did,
All of them:

Phyllis Willis, Horace Morris,
Nancy, Clancy, Bert and Gert Sturt,
Dick and Mick and Nick Crick,
Ron, Don, John,

Dolly, Molly, Polly –
Neil Peel –
And my dear old friend, Dave Dirt.

Now, I had a good time and as far as I could tell,
The party seemed to go pretty well –
Yes, that's just what it did.

Then Dad said, 'Come on, just for fun,
Let's have a *turn* from everyone!'
And a turn's just what they did,

All of them:

Phyllis Willis, Horace Morris,
Nancy, Clancy, Bert and Gert Sturt,
Dick and Mick and Nick Crick,
Ron, Don, John,
Dolly, Molly, Polly –
Neil Peel –
And my dear old friend, Dave Dirt.

AND THIS IS WHAT THEY DID:

Phyllis and Clancy
And Horace and Nancy
Did a song and dance number
That was really fancy –

Dolly, Molly, Polly,
Ron, Don and John
Performed a play
That went on and on and on –

Gert and Bert Sturt,
Sister and brother,
Did an imitation of
Each other.
(Gert Sturt put on Bert Sturt's shirt
And Bert Sturt put on Gert Sturt's skirt.)

Neil Peel
All on his own
Danced an eightsome reel.

Dick and Mick
And Nicholas Crick
Did a most *ingenious*
Conjuring trick.

And my dear old friend, Dave Dirt,
Was terribly sick
All over the flowers.
We cleaned it up.
It took *hours*.

But as Dad said, giving a party's not easy.
You really
Have to
Stick at it.
I agree. And if Dave gives a party
I'm certainly
Going to be
Sick at it.

from Queen Victoria's Diary

In Royal circles, in Victorian times, home entertainment was greatly encouraged. In 1858 Queen Victoria wrote in her diary, describing her Birthday Festivities.

After luncheon the children played:

1) Arthur and Alice, a little duet.
2) Louise: A little piece, alone, fairly, but not in time.
3) Alice and Helena, a duet – beautifully.
4) Alice and Affie on the violin – a composition of his own.
5) Alice: A long and beautiful – and very difficult – sonata by Beethoven.
6) Arthur recited a German poem.

from Making the Cat Laugh

Lynne Truss

In the new *Penguin Book of British Comic Writing* there is a short autobiographical essay by Elizabeth Bowen called 'On Not Rising to the Occasion'. I recommend it highly, especially if your memory of childhood etiquette disasters is still so vivid it makes you feel like running to the hall and burying your face in an Auntie's funny-smelling coat. Elizabeth Bowen's childhood was an Edwardian one, so she had proper guidance in suitable behaviour (she probably did not innocently repeat the word 'git' in company, as I did), but she still misjudged it sometimes in a very particular way: she 'overshot the mark'. 'Thank you, Mrs Robinson, so very, very much for the absolutely wonderful

LOVELY party!' she would say. 'Well, dear,' her hostess would reply with a frigid smile, 'I'm afraid it was hardly so wonderful as all *that*.'

My own experience of childhood parties was a little different, since I felt awkward in the society of children and generally slipped out during pass-the-parcel to ask Mrs Robinson whether I could help with the washing up – which surprised her, especially if we hadn't eaten yet. 'No, you go and have a good time,' she said, mystified, pushing me out of the kitchen with her leg. Thus, when it came to going-home time, I did not embarrass her with my effusions; I merely cried with relief. 'Lynne tried to help with the washing up,' she would inform my older sister, tapping her forehead significantly. 'Funny,' said my sister. 'She doesn't do that at home.'

But I still managed to overshoot the mark in other ways. At the age of ten, for example, I went to a party where a game of forfeits was played – you know, where you are given a task, and the penalty for failure is to kiss a boy. When my turn came (and I had been led back to the games room by a kind but firm Mrs Robinson, who declined my wild-eyed offer of silver-polishing) I was informed that my task was to recite a poem. A limerick would have easily sufficed. But I was nervous, and desperate not to kiss a boy, so I launched into 'The Highwayman', a long, galloping poem which unfortunately galloped off with me clinging on to its back, bouncing and helpless. In fact, I had got as far as '*Tlot-tlot* in the frosty silence!' before the exasperated kids finally flung themselves bodily in front of my runaway poem, waving their arms, to make me stop.

TEN COMMANDMENTS
For Being the Life of the Party

1. When you get a "bid," take it or leave it, but make up your mind.
2. Be prompt. Parties get stalled waiting for the late arrivals.
3. If asked to perform, be sure you're wanted, then do your stuff with a good grace.
4. Never hog the center of the floor after your act is done; quit while they still like you; there may be other clever people present.
5. If you can't perform, be a good audience.
6. Should the party sag, don't be afraid to volunteer first aid.
7. When asked to sing, avoid the dull stuff — better "Frankie and Johnnie" than "The Rosary."
8. Always share yourself with every one present. It is an easy road to popularity and much talent has been discovered in quiet corners.
9. Be considerate of every one in your actions and wisecracks.
10. To feel friendly, act agreeably, think charitably, and talk amusingly is to be liked by everybody, and invited everywhere.

More advice from *How to be the Life of the Party*.

Tout Ensemble

Colin West

Paula pounds the grand piano,
Vera plays the violin,
Percival provides percussion
On an empty biscuit tin.
Connie plays the concertina,
Mervyn strums the mandolin;
When you put them all together –
They make one almighty din.

from Sunny Side Up

Arthur Marshall

INDOOR GAMES

In the rainy season (September to April), I am thinking of
giving, as an alternative to Bingo, some of the Indoor Games
Parties that were so frequent in my youth. They began at 3 p.m.
(Tea, 4.30) and for these hostesses insisted on pairing
everybody off. Handed on your arrival a label with ADAM on it,
you hunted about for the girl labelled EVE ('I'm Joan Lightbody.
Who are you?'). ROMEO sought out JULIET ('Oh, hooray, Enid,
it's you!'). One's extensive knowledge of history came in useful
here and nobody announcing himself as being NELSON would
ever have dreamt of looking about for poor old Lady Nelson.

Clutching a scoring card and firmly dragooned and directed
by a hostess shrieking 'Now, all of you go and guess the smells
in the morning-room' you moved off and found yourself facing,
strung on a line across the room, a series of small opaque bags
which were being eagerly and unhygienically sniffed at by
fellow competitors. Feeling the bags was not permitted and
cheating was frowned on ('But I didn't touch it, truly, Mrs
Bumstead'). The smells were usually established fragrances such
as coffee and mint and lavender but sometimes there was a ha-
ha-ha one (pepper).

The fun was fast and furious. From a distance of twelve feet
you tried to throw playing cards into a top hat. You sucked up
peas through a straw and deposited them, with a time-limit, in
a saucer. You played that memory test, Kim's Game, with
treasured Bumstead knick-knacks set out on a tray. You
unravelled anagrams rather unfortunately referred to as
JUMBLED PARTS – ENOS, BELOW, INCH, HOT TAR, CAKE PEN.

It will be clear to ace crossword-solvers that BELOW is capable of two solutions, but ELBOW was the wise one to put down.

As the afternoon wore on, and I use the verb deliberately, it was 'Tea, everybody', and as the gingersnaps and flapjacks went down the red lanes, darkness fell, often bringing with it Colonel Bumstead ('Oh good, here's Ambrose'), a crimson-faced 'Something in the City' and who, determined to be kind and jolly, led a rumbustical game of Murder or Sardines, a pastime so graphically and memorably described by our revered Poet Laureate. On second thoughts, however, I'll give Bingo a try.

Indoor Games near Newbury

John Betjeman

In among the silver birches winding ways of tarmac wander
And the signs to Bussock Bottom, Tussock Wood and Windy
Brake,
Gabled lodges, tile-hung churches, catch the lights of our
Lagonda
As we drive to Wendy's party, lemon curd and Christmas
cake.
Rich the makes of motor whirring, past the pine-plantation
purring
Come up, Hupmobile, Delage!
Short the way your chauffeurs travel, crunching over private
gravel
Each from out his warm garage.

Oh but Wendy, when the carpet yielded to my indoor pumps
There you stood, your gold hair streaming, handsome in the
hall-light gleaming
There you looked and there you led me off into the game of
clumps
Then the new Victrola playing and your funny uncle saying
'Choose your partners for a fox-trot! Dance until its *tea*
o'clock!
'Come on, young 'uns, foot it featly!' Was it chance that
paired us neatly,
I, who loved you so completely,
You, who pressed me closely to you, hard against your party
frock?

'Meet me when you've finished eating!' So we met and no
　　one found us
Oh that dark and furry cupboard while the rest played hide
　　and seek
Holding hands our two hearts beating in the bedroom silence
　　round us
Holding hands and hardly hearing sudden footstep, thud and
　　shriek
Love that lay too deep for kissing – 'Where is Wendy?
　　Wendy's missing!'
　　　　　　　　Love so pure it *had* to end,
Love so strong that I was frighten'd when you gripped my
　　fingers tight and
　　　　　　Hugging, whispered 'I'm your friend.'

Good-bye Wendy! Send the fairies, pinewood elf and larch
　　tree gnome,
Spingle-spangled stars are peeping at the lush Lagonda
　　creeping
Down the winding ways of tarmac to the leaded lights of
　　home.
There, among the silver birches, all the bells of all the
　　churches
Sounded in the bath-waste running out into the frosty air.
Wendy speeded my undressing, Wendy is the sheet's caressing
　　　　　　Wendy bending gives a blessing,
Holds me as I drift to dreamland, safe inside my
　　slumberwear.

130

from Dainty Games

As I said in the introduction, I'm rather keen on games, so I was very pleased to find one in an antiquarian book catalogue, just in time for this book. It's from the dainty games for evening series, 1920, and you have to guess the Opera or Play. There is just room for 6 . . . answers on page 133.

WELL-KNOWN PLAY—No. 2

MA

The " Dainty " Series—No. G609   [Copyright

The "Dainty" Series—No. G609 [Copyright

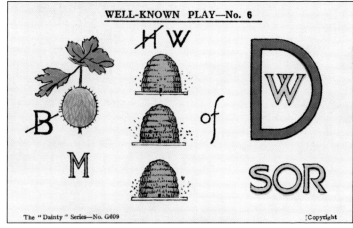

The "Dainty" Series—No. G609 [Copyright

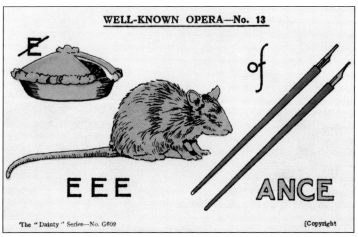

The "Dainty" Series—No. G609 [Copyright

WELL-KNOWN PLAY—No. 14

WELL-KNOWN OPERA—No. 23

The "Dainty" Series—No. G609

[Copyright

133

from Season's Greetings

Alan Ayckbourn

from Act 1, Scene i.

Christmas celebrations in the Bunker household are just beginning.

EDDIE. You – er . . . Are you going to be doing your Christmas play again this year, Bernard?

BERNARD. My puppet show? Oh yes. On Boxing Day as usual. I think I'm doing it whether I like it or not. It's become rather traditional, hasn't it? Uncle Bernard and his puppets. (*He laughs*)

EDDIE (*laughing too*). Yes. It just occurred to me, Bernard, you know, just a thought – maybe you might be thinking of jazzing it up a bit this year. I mean, I know it's a puppet show and you can't obviously do that much, I mean with all those strings and so on, but just make the story a bit more zippy, if you know what I mean? I think the kids would appreciate that. I know our three would. You should see the things they watch on TV these days. You don't mind me saying this?

BERNARD (*icily*). Has Harvey put you up to this?

EDDIE. No, no.

BERNARD. I will continue to do my puppet plays as I wish to do them and as I know children enjoy them. I think you know that I will always accept help with the manipulation but I will not have people interfering with the content of my plays. I refuse to pander. I will not include gratuitous violence or sex. Not for anyone. I will not do that. I'm sorry.

EDDIE. Who's talking about sex? I didn't mention sex.

BERNARD. I know exactly what you're talking about, don't worry.

EDDIE. I don't know why you bring sex into it.

BERNARD. I thought as a parent you might have been a little more responsible.

EDDIE. All right. All right. (*He walks into the hall with the ginger ale.*) I did not speak. I never spoke.

BERNARD (*leaving the dining-room and returning to the kitchen*). I'm disappointed, that's all I can say, I'm disappointed.

Bernard goes to the kitchen

GUESTS WE WILL NEVER INVITE AGAIN

The amateur conjurer who suddenly produces your shorts
and makes a fool of you before your guests.

The Story of Anthony,
the Boy Who Knew Too Much

Jan Struther

Anthony, though not unkind,
Had a disbelieving mind.
At a pantomime or play
Anthony would yawn and say,
'Let's go home . . . for I perceive
This is merely make believe.'
When his mother came and read
Story-books to him in bed
Anthony would shake his head:
'Mother, dear, I've had enough
Of this wishy-washy stuff.
If it's all the same to you
Kindly read me something TRUE.'
So his mother, with a sigh,
Meekly laying fiction by,
Read him books about machines,
And scientific magazines.
Christmas time came round once more.
See him sitting on the floor
At a party, after he
Has enjoyed a sumptuous tea.
Solemnly the conjuror stands
Spreading out his empty hands:
Then from nose and ears he hands
Half a dozen billiard-balls,
Shows them with a smile, and then
Makes them disappear again.
Children clap him with a will:

Only Anthony sits still,
Saying loudly, 'I believe
That he's got them up his sleeve.'

The Conjuror, who must have heard
Looked at him, but said no word.

So with all his other tricks:
Flour and butter he would mix
In a bowl, and, 'One . . . two . . . three!'
There the finished cake would be.
Loud applause . . . but Anthony
Merely said, 'Well, I believe
That he had it up his sleeve.'

Coins he'd find in Susan's hair
Which she didn't know were there;
Handkerchiefs of every hue
He would draw from Edward's shoe,
And produce, as pat as pat,
Rabbits from an empty hat.
All the other girls and boys
Laughed and clapped with merry noise:
But Anthony said, '*I* believe
He had the whole lot up his sleeve.'

The Conjuror politely smiled
At the infuriating child,
And said, 'Come close, my little man,
And learn my secrets if you can.'
Young Anthony marched up with glee
Remarking, 'Huh! You can't catch *me*!'

'Now,' said the great man, 'one-two-three!'
And Anthony . . . ah, where was he?

His mother wildly glanced around
The boy was nowhere to be found:
But in the Conjuror's top-hat
A third and extra rabbit sat . . .

Children, when you go to parties
Never talk like little smarties:
Even if you *don't* believe,
Keep your knowledge up your sleeve.

from Rebecca

Daphne du Maurier

We swerved into a main road, narrowly avoiding the car ahead of us. 'Had any people down to stay?' she asked.

'No, we've been very quiet,' I said.

'Much better, too,' she said, 'awful bore, I always think, those big parties. You won't find it alarming if you come to stay with us. Very nice lot of people all round, and we all know one another frightfully well. We dine in one another's houses, and have our bridge, and don't bother with outsiders. You do play bridge, don't you?'

'I'm not very good, Beatrice.'

'Oh, we shan't mind that. As long as you can play. I've no patience with people who won't learn. What on earth can one do with them between tea and dinner in the winter, and after dinner? One can't just sit and talk.'

I wondered why. However, it was simpler not to say anything.

'It's quite amusing now Roger is a reasonable age,' she went on, 'because he brings his friends to stay, and we have really good fun. You ought to have been with us last Christmas. We had charades. My dear, it was the greatest fun. Giles was in his element. He adores dressing-up, you know, and after a glass or two of champagne he's the funniest thing you've ever seen. We often say he's missed his vocation and ought to have been on the stage.' I thought of Giles, and his large moon face, his horn spectacles. I felt the sight of him being funny after champagne would embarrass me. 'He and another man, a great friend of ours, Dickie Marsh, dressed up as women and sang a duet. What exactly it had to do with the word in the charade nobody knew, but it did not matter. We all roared.'

GUESTS WE WILL NEVER INVITE AGAIN

"Gosh! We've gate-crashed into Uncle Fungoid's Birthday Party."

I smiled politely. 'Fancy, how funny,' I said.

I saw them all rocking from side to side in Beatrice's drawing-room. All these friends who knew one another so well. Roger would look like Giles. Beatrice was laughing again at the memory. 'Poor Giles,' she said. 'I shall never forget his face when Dick squirted the soda syphon down his back. We were all in fits.'

I had an uneasy feeling we might be asked to spend the approaching Christmas with Beatrice. Perhaps I could have influenza.

Crime Time

Anne Harvey

Sparkling Cyanide *by Agatha Christie involves two party murders.*
At the second party George suggests a toast to his wife Rosemary,
who died at the first. 'To Rosemary . . . for Remembrance'.
After a pause he sways, collapses, fights for breath.
In one and a half minutes he is dead.

There are many detective novels
Where a guest is found dead at a party,
Stabbed or strangled or smothered
As the games are growing hearty.

It happened at Pauline's party
During MURDER IN THE DARK,
Blood on the drawing room carpet!
A trick? or a joke? . . . Just a lark!

'I deduce,' said the shrewd policeman,
'This is murder; it is not a jest.
The corpse in the Butler's Pantry
Is your uninvited guest.'

But the hostess had left her party
And tiptoed upstairs to hide,
And was snuggled under the duvet
Reading SPARKLING CYANIDE.

from Nine Sharp and Earlier

Herbert Farjeon

In Herbert Farjeon's London revue Nine Sharp and Earlier,
there are sketches based on our British pastimes.
In Musical Chairs, actress Hermione Baddeley played the little girl.

(Music. Tabs part. Six people playing Musical Chairs. OLD MAN with long grey beard, YOUNG MAN, MAMA, 1ST LADY, 2ND LADY, and DUCKY (little girl) with doll. Music stops. All get seats except DUCKY, whose features, when she grasps the catastrophe, compose themselves for a howl. MAMA jumps up and hastens over to her.)

MAMA. Look, Ducky, look, *there's* a chair!
DUCKY (*still on verge of tears*). Where's a chair?
MAMA. Quick, Ducky, quick.

(DUCKY begins running in wrong direction.)

This way, Ducky. (MAMA *bundles* DUCKY *into chair, whereupon she perks up and bounces up and down.)*
DUCKY (*to* 1ST LADY). It's my birfday to-day.
1ST LADY. I know, dear.
DUCKY. I been sick twiced.
1ST LADY. I know, dear.
2ND LADY. *Isn't* she sweet?

(Music again. Five players left. OLD MAN sits down and gets up. DUCKY touches seats as she passes.)

OLD MAN (*sharply*). You mustn't touch the chairs.

DUCKY. Wasn't!

OLD MAN. You were!

DUCKY (*making face*). Gnyar!

(*Music stops. All get seats except* DUCKY, *who lets out prelude to a howl.*)

2ND LADY (*jumping up*). Where's that chair? I can't find that chair! Where *is* that chair?

MAMA. Hurry up, Ducky. (*Pushes* DUCKY *into chair.*) There we are.

DUCKY (*jeering at* 2ND LADY). You're out, sil-lee!

1ST LADY. Isn't she *sweet*?

MAMA (*to* 2ND LADY). I think she's a little over-excited.

2ND LADY. I don't wonder – *such* a booful birfday!

(*Music again. Four players left.* OLD MAN *sits down and gets up.* DUCKY *hovers.*)

OLD MAN (*sharply*). You mustn't hover.

DUCKY. Mustn't say mustn't! Boo!

OLD MAN. Don't say boo to me.

DUCKY (*stepping out of line and facing audience*). Boo-boo-boo
. . .

(*Music stops.* DUCKY *as before.* 1ST LADY *gets up, catches* DUCKY *roughly by hand, and drags her into seat.*)

1ST LADY. What a clever girlie!

DUCKY (*holding Doll against* OLD MAN'S *mouth*). Kiss my dolly! (*He kisses it.*) I love my dolly. (*Wipes doll's mouth with her handkerchief.*)

(Music again. Three players left. OLD MAN *sits down and gets up.* DUCKY *sits down.)*

OLD MAN *(sharply)*. Get up, get up.

DUCKY *(getting up)*. I am up.

OLD MAN. You *weren't* up.

DUCKY. *Who* wasn't up?

OLD MAN. *You* weren't.

DUCKY. I wasn't *what*?

(Music stops. DUCKY *as before.)*

Hermione Baddeley as Ducky and Michael Anthony as the Old Man, Little Theatre, London, 1938.

2ND LADY (*severely*). George!

YOUNG MAN (*getting up*). Sorry!

(*All rush for* DUCKY *and dump her into chair.*)

MAMA. Doesn't she love her dolly?

ALL. *Doesn't* she?

(*Music again.* OLD MAN *and* DUCKY *left.* OLD MAN *sits
down and gets up.* DUCKY *sits down and gets up.*
OLD MAN *sits down and gets up.* DUCKY *sits down and
gets up. Music stops,* OLD MAN *sits down.* DUCKY
glares at him.)

OLD MAN (*triumphantly*). I've won!

DUCKY (*smashing her doll across his head*). You bloody old
cheat!

Black Out.

Myself when Young
Alan Melville

The games one could play with any degree of safety at parties
which I attended were very limited indeed, and got fewer and
fewer as the result of one unfortunate incident after another,
until in the end we played hardly anything at all and just sat
around and sulked to the despair of the hostess. Hide the
Thimble and Hunt the Slipper were out, because if either of
these objects were hidden anywhere near any ornaments, my
exploring technique was bad for the china.

A saucy little minx who tried to kiss me.

Postman's Knock was *right* out: not because I ever overstepped the mark in kissing the little girl for whom I had a letter to deliver . . . as a matter of fact, I refused point blank to do any such thing and once drew blood by administering a sharp kick on the shinbone to a saucy little minx who tried to kiss *me*. I was, however, alleged to corrupt the morals of anyone sent out of the room to receive their letter, for the moment they came out I whisked them off to the dining-room and the pair of us had a jolly good guzzle.

Charades were a flop too. I always forgot which syllable we were supposed to be doing, and baffled the fellow-members of my team even more than the opposition. This unfortunate tendency has persisted right up to the present day. I was at a party the other night where, to the dismay of all concerned, the hostess suddenly whipped out pencils and bits of paper and announced through the hubbub that we were going to play ever such an interesting guessing game. I won't explain the details, because I didn't grasp them properly; but the gist of it was that you each had a letter in turn and had to start talking and go on talking, pretending to be someone famous whose name began with that letter. My letter was T, and I rather smugly chose a well-known Greek mathematician of the first or second century A.D. This foxed everybody, and the party broke up at around three in the morning in complete disorder. Among the foxed were, of all people, Sir Laurence and Lady Olivier, and they very kindly gave me a lift home. We were just driving away when Lady Olivier said to me in what seemed a rather chilly voice, 'And just whom were you supposed to be doing?' 'Ptolemy,' I said. 'He begins with a P,' said Lady Olivier, 'and but for you, we should have been home and in our beds two hours ago'.

Hunt the Thimble

Eleanor Farjeon

A thimble, a thimble! my Mother's gold thimble
   Is somewhere in sight if it's true what we're told.
Blue, brown, and hazel eyes, spying and prying,
   Are hunting my Mother's wee thimble of gold.

As soon as your nimble glance lights on the thimble,
   Sit down very softly and don't turn a hair.
One after other sits down, while my Mother
   Rocks backwards and forwards and smiles in her chair.

Is it perched on a picture, or propped on a statue,
  Or stuck in the keyhole instead of the key?
Oh thimble, perhaps I am looking right *at* you!
  Is *that* you? Is *that* you? Oh, where can you be?

Perhaps on the piano – the inkstand – the fender –
  Or on the brass coal-scuttle gleaming so bright?
They all have sat down! Shall I have to surrender?
  The little gold thimble is nowhere in sight.

A thimble, a thimble, my Mother's wee thimble! –
  But why as she rocks is she laughing at me?
You booby! just linger to look on my finger –
  Where else do you think that a thimble should be?

The Party

G.H. Vallins

The cakes and ale are done; I know that after,
All the dull evening long I shall deceive
My heart to mingle in the songs and laughter,
The tawdry symbols of our make-believe.

With mirth and jest the foolish spell unbroken
Shall bind me with its false and mocking power;
This paper fool's cap crown, a luckless token,
My head for one interminable hour.

The games go on: and still are you denied me –
Even one swift minute of your aching fair;
The games drag on: the music flings beside me
Not you, alas! to fill the vacant chair.

Blindfold amid the laughing throng you'll miss me,
Miss me, I know, by many a thousand mile;
And kissing all the rest you'll never kiss me,
Or paying forfeits forfeit me a smile.

Still, at the end, when we have said farewell, a
Fleeting look shall stay me at the door:
Fled from the last, mad dance my Cinderella
Shall leave one tinselled slipper on the floor.

I took my harp to a party
But nobody asked me to play,
The others were jolly and hearty
But I wasn't feeling so gay –
They might have said
'Play us a tune we can sing'
But somehow I don't think they noticed the
thing –
I took my harp to a party
But nobody asked me to play
So I took the darn thing away!
(Desmond Carter)

THE PARTY'S OVER NOW

How did the party go in Portman Square?
I cannot tell you; Juliet was not there.
And how did Lady Gaster's party go?
Juliet was next me and I do not know.

Hilaire Belloc, 'Juliet'

from Of a Party

Jan Struther

The next morning you stay in bed late, physically spent and spiritually fallow. It is all over, thank heaven: at last, at last, the party is really your own. It lies there peacefully curled up in the cradle of your memory, a rosy glamorous bundle; nothing can go wrong with it now, nothing take it from you. Occasionally you will pull down the covers, gaze at it with a glow of maternal pride, and tuck it up again: but never (you secretly swear) will you have another. Yet even as you make this vow you know that you will break it, as you have broken it so many times before.

from Trivia

Logan Pearsall Smith

SOCIAL SUCCESS

The servant gave me my coat and hat, and in a glow of self-satisfaction I walked out into the night. 'A delightful evening,' I reflected, 'the nicest kind of people. What I said about finance and French philosophy impressed them; and how they laughed when I imitated a pig squealing.'

But soon after, 'God, it's awful,' I muttered, 'I wish I were dead.'

from The History Man

Malcolm Bradbury

'A good party,' says Howard. 'A mess,' says Barbara, switching on the radio.

The radio trills, and there is a newsbreak. The noise of the radio draws the children, Martin and Celia, fresh, separate, critical beings, in their clothes from the manikin boutiques, into the kitchen; they sit down at the table, in front of coloured enamel bowls from Yugoslavia. '*Bonjour, mes amis*,' says Howard. 'Did the party make you drunk, Howard?' asks Martin. 'Who left her bra in the plantpot of the living-room geranium?' asks Celia. 'Not me,' says Howard. 'You have the messiest friends in the whole world,' says Celia. 'One of them broke a window,' says Martin, 'in the guest bedroom'. 'You've checked around, have you?' asks Howard. 'Anything else I should advise the insurance company about?' 'I think someone jumped out,' says Martin, 'there's all blood in there. Shall I go and look outside?' 'Nobody jumped out,' says Barbara. 'You sit there and eat your cornflakes.' 'Cornflakes, yuk,' says Martin. 'My compliments to the cook, and tell her "yuk",' says Howard. 'I expect this person jumped out because he couldn't stand the noise,' says Celia. 'You say *we're* noisy, but that was terrible.' 'Is there really some blood, Celia?' asks Barbara. 'Yes,' says Celia.

Party Piece

Brian Patten

He said:
'Let's stay here
Now this place has emptied
& make gentle pornography with one another,
While the partygoers go out
& the dawn creeps in,
Like a stranger.

Let us not hesitate
Over what we know
Or over how cold this place has become,
But let's unclip our minds
And let tumble free
The mad, mangled crocodiles of love.'

So they did,
Right there among the woodbines and guinness stains,
And later he caught a bus and she a train
And all there was between them then
was rain.

from Mrs Caudle's Curtain Lectures

Douglas Jerrold

Douglas Jerrold

LECTURE XIII

Mrs Caudle Has Been to See her Dear Mother.
Caudle, on the 'Joyful Occasion', Has Given a Party,
and Issued the Subjoined Card of Invitation..

'It *is* hard, I think, Mr Caudle, that I can't leave home for a day or two, but the house must be turned into a tavern: a tavern? – a pot-house!

'Yes, I thought you wanted to get rid of me for something, or you would not have insisted on my staying at dear mother's all night.

'I'm sure the house will not be sweet for a month. All the curtains are poisoned with smoke; and, what's more, with the filthiest smoke I ever knew.

'And what a condition the carpet's in! They've taken five pounds out of it, if a farthing, with their filthy boots, and I don't know what besides. And then the smoke in the hearthrug, and a large cinder hole burnt in it! I never saw such a house in *my* life! If you wanted to have a few friends, why couldn't you invite 'em when your wife's at home, like any other man? not have 'em sneaking in, like a set of housebreakers, directly a woman turns her back.

'You must all have been in a nice condition? What do you say? *You took nothing?* Took nothing, didn't you? I'm sure there's such a regiment of empty bottles, I haven't had the heart to count 'em. And punch, too! you must have punch! There's a hundred half-lemons in the kitchen, if there's one; for Susan, like a good girl, kept 'em to show 'em me. No, sir; Susan *shan't leave the house!* What do you say? *She has no right to tell tales, and you* WILL *be master of your own house?* Will you? If you don't alter, Mr Caudle, you'll soon have no house to be master of. A whole loaf of sugar did I leave in the cupboard, and now there isn't as much as would fill a tea-cup. Do you suppose I'm to find sugar for punch for fifty men? What do you say? *There*

Mr. Caudle's compliments to Mr. Henry Prettyman, and expects to have the honour of his company on this joyful occasion, at half-past Eight o'Clock.

wasn't fifty? That's no matter; the more shame for 'em, sir. I'm sure they drunk enough for fifty.

'No, I *won't* be still: and I *won't* let you go to sleep. If you'd got to bed at a proper hour last night, you wouldn't have been so sleepy now. You can sit up half the night with a pack of people who don't care for you, and your poor wife can't get in a word!

'And there's that China image that I had when I was married – I wouldn't have taken any sum of money for it, and you know it – and how do I find it? With its precious head knocked off! And what was more mean, more contemptible than all besides, it was put on again, as if nothing had happened. *You knew nothing about it?* Now, how can you lie there, in your Christian bed, Caudle, and say that? You know that that fellow,

Prettyman, knocked off the head with the poker? You know that he did. And you hadn't the feeling, – yes, I will say it, – you hadn't the feeling to protect what you knew was precious to me. Oh no, if the truth was known, you were glad to see it broken for that very reason.

'Every way, I've been insulted. I should like to know who it was who corked whiskers on my dear aunt's picture? Oh! you're laughing, are you? *You're not laughing?* Don't tell me that. I should like to know what shakes the bed, then, if you're not laughing? Yes, corked whiskers on her dear face, – and she was a good soul to you, Caudle, and you ought to be ashamed of yourself to see her ill-used. Oh, you may laugh! It's very easy to laugh! I only wish you'd a little feeling, like other people, that's all.

'There's four glasses broke and nine cracked. At least, that's all I've found out at present; but I dare say I shall discover a dozen to-morrow.

'And I should like to know where the cotton umbrella's gone to – and I should like to know who broke the bell-pull – and perhaps you don't know there's a leg off a chair, – and perhaps –'

'I was resolved,' says Caudle, 'to know nothing, and so went to sleep in my ignorance.'

Ballade of Soporific Absorption

J.C. Squire

Ho! Ho! Yes! Yes! It's very all well,
    You may drunk I am think, but I tell you I'm not,
I'm as sound as a fiddle and fit as a bell,
    And stable quite ill to see what's what.

I under *do* stand you surprise a got
When I headed my smear with gooseberry jam:
    And I've swallowed, I grant, a beer of lot –
But I'm not so think as you drunk I am.

Can I liquor my stand? Why, yes, like hell!
    I care not how many a tossed I've pot
I shall stralk quite weight and not yutter an ell,
    My feech will not spalter the least little jot:
    If you knownly had own! – well, I gave him a dot,
And I said to him, 'Sergeant, I'll come like a lamb –
    The floor it seems like a storm in a yacht,
But I'm not so think as you drunk I am.'

When I was at the Party

Anon

'When I was at the party,'
   Said Betty, aged just four,
'A little girl fell off her chair
   Right down upon the floor;
And all the other little girls
   Began to laugh, but me –
I didn't laugh a single bit,'
   Said Betty seriously.

'Why not?' her mother asked her,
   Full of delight to find
That Betty – bless her little heart! –
   Had been so sweetly kind.
'Why didn't you laugh, my darling?
   Or don't you like to tell?'
'I didn't laugh,' said Betty,
   ''Cause it was me that fell.'

from Of Uncles and Aunts

Bettina

'That's a nice little boy! I like him. Who's he?'

'That is my cousin Leopold, Poldi for short. Here he was dressed up as a little Cupid in pink satin and white wig and with bow and arrows to go to a fancy-dress ball.

'But when he got there he found that he was much the youngest and smallest person and the only one who could not dance. After watching the others for a while he suddenly burst out in tears crying: "Nobody dance with Poldi!"

'But my mother heard it and whirled him into a dance; then she secretly took him to the room where all the food was waiting and he ate half a chocolate cake and then fell asleep in an armchair sighing: "Poldi enjoyed the party more than *anyone* else!"'

'I'm glad he did!'

'Footman Quartette'
from Bitter Sweet

Noël Coward

Now the party's really ended,
And our betters have ascended,
All with throbbing heads,
To their welcome beds,
Pity us, who have to be up,
Sadly clearing the debris up,
Getting for our pains
Most of the remains.

Though the Major-Domo is a trifle tight,
Though the mistress hiccoughed when she said
    good night,
We in our secluded garret,

Mean to finish up the claret
Cup all right.
When we've doused the final candles,
We'll discuss the latest scandals
We have overheard,
Pleasure long deferred.
When the Duke of So-and-So stares
At his wife, we know below stairs,
While she smirks and struts,
That he hates her guts.
Though we all disguise our feelings pretty well,
What we mean by 'Very good' is 'Go to hell'.
Though they're all so grand and pompous,
Most of them are now non compos,
Serve them right,
Good night.

ABOUT THE AUTHORS AND ILLUSTRATORS

Nicholas Allan (b. 1956). Writer and illustrator of picture books. *Hilltop Hospital* was filmed and won the 2003 BAFTA Award. Other prizes: Sheffield Children's Book Award (1994) and the Children's Book Award (2000).

Alan Ayckbourn (b. 1939). Popular contemporary playwright and artistic director of the Theatre in the Round, Scarborough, Yorks. He received a knighthood in 1997.

Hilaire Belloc (1870–1953). Poet, critic, politician, of French Catholic ancestry, who wrote on a wide range of subjects, including *Cautionary Tales* (1907), which has never been out of print.

Nicolas Bentley (1907–78). Artist, journalist and writer. A popular contributor to *Punch*, *Sunday Times*, *Daily Mail* and *Private Eye* and illustrator of many books, including his own classic *How can you Bear to be Human* (Deutsch, 1957).

John Betjeman (1906–84). Much-loved writer, poet and broadcaster on English life, places and people. He received a knighthood in 1969 and became Poet Laureate in 1972.

Malcolm Bradbury (1932–2000). Critic and novelist. His last academic appointment was as Professor of American Studies at the University of East Anglia.

Simon Brett (b. 1945). Writer, dramatist, editor and broadcaster, well known for his popular crime novels and radio series. A former chairman of the Crime Writers' Association.

Alan Brownjohn (b. 1931). Poet, critic, novelist, teacher. In 1990 he won the Authors' Club Award for his novel *The Way You Tell Them*. His most recent poetry is published by Enitharmon Press.

Frances Hodgson Burnett (1849–1924). Best known for her children's books *Little Lord Fauntleroy*, *The Secret Garden* and *A Little Princess*, all made into films and plays.

Lord Byron (1788–1824). One of Britain's most famous poets and equally popular in Europe and America. His letters and journals are vivid commentaries on his life and times.

William Chappell (1907–94). Dancer and theatre designer who worked with the Vic Wells and Rambert ballet companies.

Susanna Clarke (b. 1959). Her first novel, *Jonathan Strange & Mr Norrell*, received much praise and was long-listed for the Booker and short-listed for the Whitbread Prizes in 2004.

Enid Clay (b. 1881). Poet, and sister of the artist Eric Gill, who illustrated her collection of poetry, *Sonnets & Verses* (1925).

Noël Coward (1899–1973). Actor, dramatist, composer and much-loved twentieth-century theatre personality, affectionately known as 'The Master'. He received a knighthood in 1970.

Mrs Craik (Diana Maria Mulock) (1826–87). Novelist and poet, best known for her book *John Halifax, Gentleman*. She donated her Civil List Pension for less fortunate writers.

E.M. Delafield (1890–1943). The pen name of Edmée Elizabeth Monica Dashwood, writer of many popular novels, besides her

Provincial Lady titles. She was a director of the magazine *Time & Tide*.

Charles Dickens (1812–70). Began his working life by writing articles, short stories and serials for many publications. Became one of the most popular writers, worldwide, of all time.

Margaret Drabble (b. 1939). Novelist and biographer. She edited *A Writer's Britain* and *The Oxford Companion to English Literature*, and was awarded the CBE for Services to English Literature in 1980.

Daphne du Maurier (1907–89). Novelist and dramatist. Many of her books are set in Cornwall and have been adapted for film, stage and radio. She was made a Dame in 1969.

Bettina Ehrlich (b. 1903). Studied Art in her native Austria before moving to London. Wrote and illustrated many books for children, including *Of Aunts and Uncles* (1963). She worked under the name Bettina.

T.S. Eliot (1888–1965). American-born poet, critic and dramatist, whose poetry and verse dramas broke new ground. A director of the publisher Faber & Faber, he was awarded the Nobel Prize for Literature and the Order of Merit in 1948.

Eleanor Farjeon (1881–1965). Writer, poet, dramatist of over eighty titles, including *Kings and Queens* in collaboration with her brother Herbert, and *The Little Bookroom* (1955). She was awarded the Hans Andersen, Carnegie and Regina (US) prizes, and an annual award is given in her name.

Herbert Farjeon (1887–1945). Theatre critic, dramatist, lyricist and director of West End revues. As a journalist he contributed to many journals, wrote on cricket, and edited the Nonesuch Shakespeare.

Helen Fielding (b. 1958). Writer and journalist. Produced BBC documentaries for Comic Relief. Both *Bridget Jones's Diary*

(1996) and *Bridget Jones: The Edge of Reason* (1999) became popular films.

Anne Harriet Fish (1890–1964). Contributed to American and English magazines. Illustrated the books of othr writers, as well as her own *Awful Weekends & Guests* (1938) and *All's Well that Ends Well* (1939).

Virginia Graham (1910–93). Poet, journalist and critic. Contributed to *Punch* and other periodicals and in 1946–56 was film critic for the *Spectator*. She sometimes wrote material for her friend Joyce Grenfell.

Joyce Grenfell (1910–79). One of the best-loved British stage, film and radio entertainers. As well as songs, sketches and poems, she wrote two volumes of autobiography, and her wartime journals.

Charlotte Guest (1812–95). Translated the *Mabinogian* from medieval Welsh, had twelve children, and helped her second husband to acquire eighteenth-century ceramics that are now in the V&A's Schreiber Collection.

Alec Guinness (1914–2000). Actor and writer. In addition to his memorable theatre performances, he acted in many films, winning an Oscar for *The Bridge on the River Kwai*. He wrote three volumes of autobiography and received his knighthood in 1994.

A.P. Herbert (1890–1971). A versatile writer of novels, stage musicals and witty, humorous poetry who campaigned for many causes, was MP for Oxford University 1935–50, and was knighted in 1945.

Haro Hodson (b. 1923). Illustrator and cartoonist who was an official war artist during the Second World War. His work has appeared in many magazines and newspapers, including *Punch* and the *Daily Mail*.

Thomas Hood (1799–1845). Despite ill-health, a prolific writer of satire, parody and humour, and a master of the pun. He also wrote many serious poems including 'The Song of the Shirt' and 'The Dream of Eugene Aram'.

Kenneth Horne. Writer and popular broadcaster of many programmes, most notably of the much-loved *Round the Horne*, which is now part of twentieth-century British culture, and has a large following today.

Agnes Jekyll (1860–1937). Lived at Munstead House in Surrey, near to her sister-in-law, the famous garden designer Gertrude Jekyll. An excellent hostess, who was created DBE for her involvement in many good causes.

Elizabeth Jennings (1926–2001). Critic and poet of over twenty collections. A lifelong Catholic, she was inspired by religion, the Arts and people. Among many distinctions were an Arts Council and W.H. Smith Award and the CBE in 1987.

Douglas Jerrold (1803–57). Writer and dramatist, well known in theatre circles and for his contributions to *Punch*, where *Mrs Caudle's Curtain Lectures* first appeared. His best-known play is *Black-Ey'd Susan*.

Mary Killen. As a writer and humorist she made her mark on the *Tatler* and for several years was author of the 'Bystander' Social pages. She contributes to many other periodicals, including the *Oldie*.

John Lawrence (b. 1933). Illustration, in pen and water colour, of over 100 books. Fellow of the Royal Society of Printmakers and Society of Wood Engravers, and in 1990 Master of the Art Workers' Guild. He has twice won the Francis Williams Book Illustration Award.

Helen Lederer. Actor, writer and presenter of Radio 4 programmes. Theatre work includes *Educating Rita* and *The Vagina Monologues*, and numerous TV appearances include *Absolutely Fabulous* and *The Harry Enfield Show*.

John Leech (1817–64). Artist and illustrator. Contributed satirical and political lithographs for *Punch* and other magazines, and illustrated the work of Trollope, Jerrold, Dickens and most notably R.S. Surtees.

Sylvia Lynd (1888–1952). Novelist, poet and short-story writer, married to the Irish critic and essayist Robert Lynd. A member of the Vie Heureuse and Book Society Committees in the 1920s.

Rose Macaulay (1881–1958). Novelist, essayist and travel writer. Her best-known books include *They Were Defeated* (1932), *The World My Wilderness* (1950) and *Crewe Train* (1992).

Katherine Mansfield (1888–1923). Came to England from her native New Zealand in 1902. Married editor-writer John Middleton Murry, and was part of an artistic, literary group. Wrote poetry and short stories.

Arthur Marshall (1910–89). Writer, journalist and broadcaster. Housemaster at his old school, Oundle, then Private Secretary to Lord Rothschild. Among his books are *Girls Will Be Girls*, *Giggling in the Shrubbery* and an autobiography, *Life's Rich Pageant*.

Jan Martin (b. 1932). Trained at Hornsey and Norwich Schools of Art and worked in teaching and as a book illustrator. As curator of the Halesworth Art Gallery in Suffolk, she promotes the work of other East Anglian artists.

Judith Martin. American writer, known as 'Miss Manners' through her *Guides to Rearing Perfect Children* (1984) and *Excruciatingly Good Behaviour*. Also wrote novels.

Elsa Maxwell (1883–1963). Compulsive American party-giver and gossip columnist. Well known in theatrical circles and on first nights . . . not always for the best reasons.

Phyllis McGinley (1905–78). American poet and humorist who won a Pulitzer Prize in 1960 for her book of light verse, *Times Three*.

Roger McGough (b. 1937). Poet, critic, editor and broadcaster. One of the group known as the 'Liverpool Poets', he has published many collections. He presents Radio 4's *Poetry Please*, and has received many awards, and, in 1997, the OBE.

Alan Melville (1910–83). Revue writer, author and broadcaster, who worked at the BBC in Features and Drama. As well as London revues, he wrote plays and musicals and two autobiographies, *Myself when Young* and *Merely Melville*.

Charlotte Mitchell. Author of three collections of poetry. She has also worked as an actress, appearing in theatre, television, cinema and on radio.

John Mole (b. 1941). Teacher, poet, critic and jazz musician. He has received the Signal and Cholmondeley Awards for poetry, and is Poet-in-Residence for the City of London.

George Morrow (1869–1955). Illustrator of many books, among them A.P. Herbert's *Laughing Ann* and, for children, F.G. Evans's *Puffin, Puma & Company*, as well as *George Morrow his Book* (1920) and *More Morrow* (1921).

Ogden Nash (1902–71). American poet of sophisticated, witty verse for adults and children, known for puns, epigrams and quirky rhymes.

Jeremy Nicholas (b. 1947). Actor, writer, broadcaster and musician. His solo performance of Jerome K. Jerome's *Three Men in a Boat* was nominated for an Oscar, and in 1996 he won the Sony Gold Award for best arts programme.

Brian Patten (b. 1946). Poet, dramatist, storyteller and editor. His adult poetry is translated into several languages. One of the Liverpool poets, he won a special award from the Mystery Writers of America Guild for his book *Mr Moon's Last Case*.

Raymond Peynet (1908–99). Well-loved French cartoonist who contributed to many magazines and also designed for theatre. He won the Grand Prix at an International Festival of Humour.

Cole Porter (1891–1964). Legendary American composer-lyricist. Known for many film and theatre successes on Broadway, in London and worldwide, among them *Kiss Me Kate*, *Anything Goes* and *High Society*.

Margaret Powell (1907–84). Writer who worked in domestic service before and after the Second World War. Her fine observation, wit and humour are shown in *Below Stairs* and other books about her working life.

Winthrop Mackworth Praed (1802–39). Founded *The Etonian*, his school magazine, was called to the bar, and entered Parliament as Secretary to the Board of Trade. Best known for his elegant and witty *vers de société*.

Alan Pryce-Jones (1908–2000). Critic, author and journalist. Before the war he was assistant editor of the London Mercury, and editor of the *Times Literary Supplement* in 1948–59. He wrote two musicals and an autobiography.

Hermione Ranfurley (1913–2001). Writer and one-time confidential secretary to the Head of Special Operations Executive in Cairo. She founded what is now the Book Aid Foundation and was appointed OBE in 1970.

Gwen Raverat (1885–1959). Artist and wood engraver. A grand-daughter of Charles Darwin, in 1952 she wrote *Period Piece: A Cambridge Childhood*, which has never been out of print.

Tony Ross (b. 1938). Worked in advertising and taught art at Manchester Polytechnic. One of the most popular illustrators of picture books, he has won many awards internationally.

Albert Rutherston (1881–1953). Painter and illustrator, and Ruskin Master at Oxford 1929–1949. Books he illustrated include *The Children's Bluebird* (1913), *Mr Marionette* (1925) and *The Weekend Book* (1924).

Siegfried Sassoon (1886–1967). Poet and writer. Won the Military Cross in the First World War but threw it away in his contempt for war. In 1919 became Literary Editor of the *Daily Herald*. His two autobiographies won the Hawthornden and the James Tait Black Memorial Prizes, and he received the CBE in 1951.

Emily Shore (1819–39). A keen naturalist and ornithologist with a love of learning, she began writing her journals at 11, continuing until her death, from consumption, in Madeira, aged 19.

Norman Silver (b. 1946). Poet and novelist. Born in Cape Town, South Africa, he moved to England in 1969. As well as his poetry collections, he has published two novels.

Posy Simmonds (b. 1945). Studied painting and graphic design in Paris and London in the 1970s. She is well known for her witty outlook on family and literary life, and contributes a satirical comic strip to the *Guardian*.

Nigel Slater. Writer of best-selling books on food as well as a popular column for the *Observer*. Described as 'a national treasure', his book *Toast* won the W.H. Smith People's Choice, the André Simon and the British Books Biography awards for 2003.

Logan Pearsall Smith (1805–1946). An American who lived in England, and was a founder of The Society for Pure English. His witty, polished collections include *Trivia* (1902), *More Trivia* (1921) and *Afterthoughts* (1931).

J.C. Squire (1884–1958). Literary journalist, editor and poet. Established the *London Mercury*, and was Literary Editor of the *New*

Statesman and chief literary critic on the *Observer*. His literary coterie was called the 'Squirearchy'. He was knighted in 1933.

Jan Struther (1901–53). The pseudonym for Joyce Maxtone-Graham. Her column for the court page of *The Times* led to her book *Mrs Miniver*, later a popular film. As well as her journalism, she published collections of poetry, including *The Modern Struwwelpeter*, first seen in *Punch*.

Annie Tempest. Contributor to all the major national newspapers and lifestyle magazines, who has had fourteen one-woman shows. Her entire range, under the heading 'Tottering-by-Gently-in-Mayfair', has a room at the O'Shea Gallery, SW1.

Anthony Thwaite (b. 1930). A university teacher in Japan and Libya, a BBC Radio producer, literary editor of the *Listener* and *New Statesman*, and co-editor of *Encounter*. He has received the Richard Hillary Memorial and Cholmondeley awards and the OBE for services to poetry.

Anthony Trollope (1815–1882). Hugely successful novelist of 47 titles, as well as biographies, short stories and sketches. Many of his novels have been successfully dramatised. Started work in the Civil Service.

Lynne Truss (b. 1955). Writer, critic and broadcaster. She won the Columnist of the Year Award for her work on *Woman's Journal*. *Eats, Shoots & Leaves*, her best-selling book on punctuation, was published in 2003.

G.H. Vallins. Well known for editing lively books and school textbooks on the English Language and was a regular contributor to *John o' London's Weekly*, *Punch* and the *Radio Times*.

Queen Victoria (1819–1901). Many selections from the Queen's letters and diaries (there were 100 volumes of these) have been published, offering insight into her family life.

Judith Viorst. American poet, first published in the magazines *New York* and *Nova*. She has written two musicals, non-fiction and fifteen children's books.

Evelyn Waugh (1903–66). A successful novelist, journalist and travel writer, who started work as a teacher and also served in the Royal Navy in the war. As well as many novels, his diaries (1976) and autobiography (1964) are revealing.

Colin West (b. 1951). Poet, storyteller and illustrator, known for his witty, quirky wordplay and humorous pictures. He has published over fifty titles and a collection, *The Big Book of Nonsense*, came out in 2001.

Oscar Wilde (1854–1900). Writer, dramatist and poet, who attracted attention with his flamboyant appearance and aestheticism. His plays are always in performance. Wilde was imprisoned for homosexual offences, and released in 1898.

Bob Wilson (b. 1942). Worked extensively for many years in the advertising world, latterly as an art director. His work appeared in *Punch*, the *Times* supplements and *The Cartoonist*, and is often seen on the cover of *The Oldie*. Winner of a Heinemann Book Award.

Kit Wright (b. 1944). Poet, critic and editor. Among many honours, he has been awarded the Hawthornden Prize, the Royal Society of Literature's Heinemann Prize and the Geoffrey Faber Memorial Award.

Anna Zinkeisen (1901–76). Painter and illustrator who exhibited at the Royal Academy, and in the 1930s designed posters for London Transport. Her stylish illustrations enhanced many books.

ACKNOWLEDGEMENTS

I have many people to thank for their interest and assistance during the making of *Party Pieces*. Among them are my two editors at Sutton Publishing, Jaqueline Mitchell and Hilary Walford, for their patient support of a non-computerised anthologist. And also the following: Saeid Ansari-Saeid at Digital Picture & Print, Bee and Walter Wyeth and the staff of Pitshanger Bookshop, Amelia Cherry, Richard Furstenheim, Philip Glassborow, Frances Guthrie, Janie Hampton, Colin Pinney, Mary Sergeant and Colin West. Their help has been invaluable.

The editor and publishers gratefully acknowledge permission to reprint copyright material in this book as follows:

Nicholas Allan: extracts from *The Complete Guide to Gatecrashing* (Ebury Press, 2001), copyright © Nicholas Allan. Reprinted with the author's permission.

Alan Ayckbourn: extract from *Season's Greetings*, copyright © 1982 by Haydonning Ltd. Published by Samuel French, 1982.

All rights whatsoever in this play are strictly reserved and application for performance etc. must be made before rehearsal to Casarotto Ramsay Ltd, National House, 60–66 Wardour Street, London W1V 4ND. No performance may be given unless a licence has been obtained.

Hilaire Belloc: extract from *Complete Verse* by Hilaire Belloc. Reprinted by permission of PfD on behalf of the Estate of Hilaire Belloc, copyright © Estate of Hilaire Belloc, 1970.

Elizabeth Jennings: for permission to reproduce 'A Company of Friends' by Elizabeth Jennings (*Collected Poems*, Carcanet Press, 2002), David Higham Associates on behalf of the copyright holder.

Mary Killen: for extracts from *Best Behaviour* by Mary Killen published by Century. Reprinted by permission of the Random House Group Ltd.

Helen Lederer: for permission to reproduce an extract from *Coping* by Helen Lederer (Angus & Robertson, 1988), copyright © the author.

Sylvia Lynd: for an extract from *Eat, Drink & Be Merry*, copyright © The Estate of Sylvia Lynd.

Judith Martin: for extracts from *Miss Manners' Guide to Excruciatingly Good Behaviour* (Penguin Books), copyright © 2005, United Feature Syndicate, Inc.

Roger McGough: for permission to reproduce the poem 'May Ball' from *Holiday on Death Row* (1979), the author, copyright © Roger McGough.

Alan Melville: for an extract from *Myself when Young* (Max Parrish, 1955), permission to reprint Eric Glass Ltd, London, for the author's Estate.

Charlotte Mitchell: for the poem 'Party' from *I Want to Go Home* (Souvenir Press, 1990), copyright © the author.

John Mole: for the poem 'Nel Mezzo del Cammin' by John Mole, copyright © the author.

Ogden Nash: for 'The Darkest Half-hour' from *Candy is Dandy* by Ogden Nash with an introduction by Anthony Burgess (André

Deutsch, Ltd). Permission granted by Carlton Books Ltd on behalf of the author's estate.

Jeremy Nicholas: for permission to reprint 'Place Settings', a song published by Novello & Company in *Sarah's Encores*, copyright © Jeremy Nicholas.

Brian Patten: for the poem 'Party Piece' from *Little Johnny's Confession* (Unwin, 1967/87), copyright © the author.

Cole Porter: for 'The Extra Man'. Words & Music by Cole Porter from Words & Music Copyright © 1977 CP Music, Inc, USA. Warner Chappell Music Ltd, London W6 8BS.

Countess of Ranfurly: for an extract from *The Ugly One* copyright © Estate of Hermione Ranfurly 1988, by permission of PfD on behalf of the Estate of Hermione Ranfurly.

Gwen Raverat: for an extract from *Period Piece* (Faber, 1952), copyright © The Estate of Gwen Raverat.

Siegfried Sassoon: for an extract from *The Old Century* by Siegfried Sassoon. Copyright © Siegfried Sassoon, used by permission of Viking Penguin, a division of The Penguin Group (USA) Inc. Also copyright by kind permission of George Sassoon & Barbara Levy Literary Agency, London.

Norman Silver: for the poem 'My Party' from *Words on a Faded T-Shirt* (Faber 1991), copyright © the author.

Nigel Slater: for 'Birthday Cake' from *Toast* by Nigel Slater copyright © the author 2003. Reprinted by permission of Lucas Alexander Whitley Ltd on behalf of Harper Collins (publishers).

Jan Struther: for 'The Story of Anthony, the Boy Who Knew Too Much' from *The English Struwwelpeter*, permission Punch Library;

and for an extract from *Of a Party* by Jan Struther, the Jan Struther Estate, copyright © the Jan Struther Estate.

Anthony Thwaite: for the poem 'My Oxford' from *A Portion for Foxes* (OUP, 1977), copyright © the author.

Lynne Truss: for an extract from *Making the Cat Laugh* by Lynne Truss published by Profile Books, permission granted by David Higham Associates, copyright © the author.

Judith Viorst: for permission to reproduce the poem 'Cocktail Party' from *It's Hard to be Hip over Thirty* (Persephone Books Ltd), copyright © Judith Viorst.

Colin West: for poems and illustrations from *The Big Book of Nonsense* (2001), copyright © Colin West.

Kit Wright: for his poem 'My Party' from *Rabbiting On* (William Collins Sons & Co. Ltd, 1978), copyright © the author.

PICTURE CREDITS

Nicolas Bentley: p. 12, from *The Diary of a Provincial Lady* (Folio Society, 1979), copyright © Curtis Brown Ltd on behalf of the Estate of Nicolas Bentley.

Haro Hodson: p. 63, from *True to Type* by Denys Parsons (Macdonald, 1955), and p. 146, from *Myself when Young* (Max Parrish, 1955), copyright © the artist.

John Lawrence: p. 99, from *Entertaining with Cranks* (J.M. Dent, 1985), copyright © John Lawrence.

Jan Martin: pp. 54 and 55, for illustrations to 'Johnnie! Me and You', copyright © the artist.

Raymond Peynet: p. 80, from *The Lovers' Keepsake* (Perpetua, 1958), ADAGP, Paris and DACS, London, 2005.

Gwen Raverat: p. 107, from *The Bedside Barsetshire* (Faber, 1959), copyright © Estate of Gwen Raverat 2005. All rights reserved, DACS, London.

Tony Ross: pp. 94, 95 and 96, from *Not Another Little Sod* (Orion, 1995), copyright © Tony Ross.

Posy Simmonds: pp. 120 and 122, from *Rabbiting On* by Kit Wright (William Collins Sons & Co. Ltd, 1978), copyright © the artist.

Annie Tempest: p. 73, from *Best Behaviour* by Mary Killen (Century, 1990), copyright © Annie Tempest at The O'Shea Gallery, London.

Colin West: pp. 68 and 126, from *The Big Book of Nonsense* (Hutchinson, 2001), copyright © the artist.

Bob Wilson: p. 92, cover illustration from the *Oldie* (September 2003), permission Bob Wilson and the *Oldie*, copyright © Bob Wilson.

Anna Zinkeisen: pp. 18 and 160, from *The Years of Grace* (Evans, 1950), and pp. 85, 105 and 163, from *A Book of Ballads: A.P. Herbert's Light Verse* (Benn, 1931), copyright © Julia Heseltine for the Estate of Anna Zinkeisen.

Also Bettina (pp. 161, 162), Reginald Birch (p. 103), William Chappell (pp. 1, 21) from *The Pleasure of your Company* (Howe, 1933), Anne Harriet Fish 'Fish' (pp. 29, 75, 135, 140) from *Awful Weekends & Guests* (Methuen, 1938), Beryl Irving (pp. 19, 36, 102, 138) from *The Family Weekend Book* (Seeley, Service & Co. Ltd, n.d.), John Leech (pp. 71, 155, 157), George Morrow (p. 159), Helen Read (p. 48) from *A Picnic of Poetry* edited by Anne Harvey (Blackie, 1988), Albert Rutherston (pp. 117, 149) from *The Week-End Book* (Nonesuch Press, 1928), Reginald Woolley (pp. 59, 82) from *The Two Bouquets* (Michael Joseph, 1948). The illustrations on pp. 16 and 89 are from *The Christmas Book* (Sampson Low, n.d.). Illustrations on pp. 10, 119 and 125 are from *How to be the Life of the Party: A Handy Guide to a Good Time for those who Want a Little Whooppee in their Homes* by Edward Longstreth, illustrated by SCHUS (Modern Sports Publishing Co., 1931).

All other illustrations and photographs are from the editor's own collection of archive material, cuttings and memorabilia.

While every effort has been made to secure permission, in a few cases it has been impossible to trace the copyright holder. In such cases we would be pleased to include the correct form of copyright in future editions.

INDEX OF AUTHORS